# SOFT FURNISHINGS

Using beautiful fabrics and trimmings
to embellish your furniture and home

# SOFT FURNISHINGS

p

This is a Parragon Publishing Book
This edition published in 2003

Parragon Publishing
Queen Street House
4 Queen Street
Bath BA1 1HE, UK



Created and produced for Parragon by The Bridgewater Book Company Ltd.

*Creative Director* Stephen Knowlden
*Art Director* Michael Whitehead
*Designer* Alistair Plumb
*Editorial Director* Fiona Biggs
*Editor* Nicola Wright
*Photography* Steve Tanner
*Picture Researcher* Lynda Marshall
*Styling* Jack Britton

ISBN: 0-75257-165-6

Printed in China

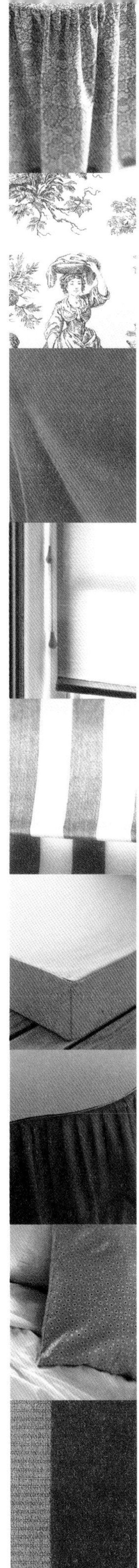

# Contents

# introduction

Making soft furnishings may not be as daunting as you think. With a little imagination, determination, and some background knowledge of the basic techniques, you will be surprised at how easy it is. With a little practice even a complete beginner can begin to create furnishings that will enhance the home.

The soft furnishings you choose for your home play a very important role in its decor, helping to set the "mood" each room creates: make the right choice and the feeling will be warm and welcoming, but if you get it wrong, you will make the room cold and uninviting. So always choose soft furnishings with great care, bearing in mind the overall effect they will produce when they are combined.

Of course, you can simply go out and buy the soft furnishings you need for each room—curtains, cushions, table linen, bed linen, and so on—and there is no doubt that there are many lovely items to choose from, but if you do that, you're always going to be limited by someone else's idea of pattern, material, size, and shape, and that may mean making compromises. If you want to achieve effects that are far more unique and completely in tune with your decorative theme, you will be far better off making your own, or altering ready-made items. What's more, making something yourself has other advantages too. For example, fabrics come in a kaleidoscope of different colors, patterns, weights, and textures, providing much greater versatility when it comes to finding exactly what you want. By using your imagination, you may find that you can use certain fabrics in a way that would not make sense commercially, but that gives you just the effect you're looking for. Making something yourself can be very satisfying, too—while you're making it and when you've finished—but the biggest bonus of all is that it will save you money.

While making your own soft furnishings will allow you to tailor them to your exact needs to fit in with your planned decor, and match any special requirements as to size, you can also use your sewing skills to give a new lease of life to a variety of old or plain items of furniture. These can be fitted with new covers for a fresh look, or perhaps made more comfortable with extra padding or cushions.

The important thing to remember is that making soft furnishings is not as difficult as you may think, and the techniques and projects in this book will show you exactly how to achieve the most impressive results throughout your home. And once you have gained the basic skills, you will be able to add your own embellishments to the designs to make items that are truly unique and exactly right for your home.

Choosing the right fabric for a project is the cornerstone of success, and our guide to furnishing fabrics will give you a good insight into what's available and how it can be used. You'll also find useful tips on handling and cleaning particular types of fabric.

Sewing, like any other practical task, can only be completed successfully if you have the right equipment, and we'll tell you all the things you need. Make sure you have everything required before starting a project; it's infuriating to have to break off because you're missing something vital.

If you're a complete beginner, we'll show you how to make patterns and cut out fabric, together with a range of basic sewing skills that will set you on the road to success. You'll be surprised at how easy it is and how much you'll be able to achieve with practice.

Subsequent sections of the book deal with specific types of soft furnishing—curtains and blinds, cushions and seat covers, tablecloths and table linen, and bed linen. By following the techniques and projects they describe, you'll be able to create the most wonderful soft furnishings to suit perfectly every room in your home.

***Creating your own soft furnishings can transform old furniture, giving it a new lease of life in a style that is unique to your home.***

# getting started

The success of any soft furnishing project depends very much on three vital elements: the right material, the right equipment, and the appropriate skills. The following pages will show you how to ensure all three.

Choice of fabric is very much a personal matter, but there are important points to consider. You need to ask yourself: can you live with your choice of fabric in the long term? And just as important: is the fabric up to the job?

Sewing will be much easier, and the results much more pleasing, if you have the right equipment, so be prepared to invest a little; you won't regret it. As for skills, you'll be surprised at what you can achieve with a little practice.

# choosing fabrics

Choosing a furnishing fabric is a decision that mustn't be rushed. You may want to live with your choice for many years, so the fabric needs to be a pleasure to look at, as well as being practical. Follow your instincts rather than current trends. Enhance favorite items bought on foreign travels with ethnic, patterned fabrics or colors.

Always get samples to look at in situ; maybe buy 19in/0.5m of the fabric to be certain it is right for you. View the fabric in both daylight and electric light, and place it in its intended position. Sit on it if it is to be used for seating: see if it crushes easily and would therefore look creased and tattered very quickly. Drape curtains at a window. Look in from outside your window at night to see how much privacy they offer. See how the color looks combined with those already in the room. Take care when mixing patterns—they may all co-ordinate well together, but not be restful to live with on a day-to-day basis. Up-to-the-minute fabrics are very covetable but will date, so use them for smaller items, such as cushions and lampshades. Buy the best-quality fabric that your budget allows, and it will repay you by lasting longer.

## *Furnishing fabric checklist*

### Brocade

Originally made of silk, this luxurious fabric is now always made from synthetic fibers. Swirling, raised designs, often incorporating metal threads, are very characteristic of a typical brocade design. Brocade frays easily, so work double hems and neaten any seams. Use for curtains, upholstery, and cushions.

### Broderie anglaise

This lightweight cotton, or cotton and polyester-mix fabric has delicate designs punched out and then embroidered. The embroidery is often worked along a border, making it very effective on bed-linen and curtains.

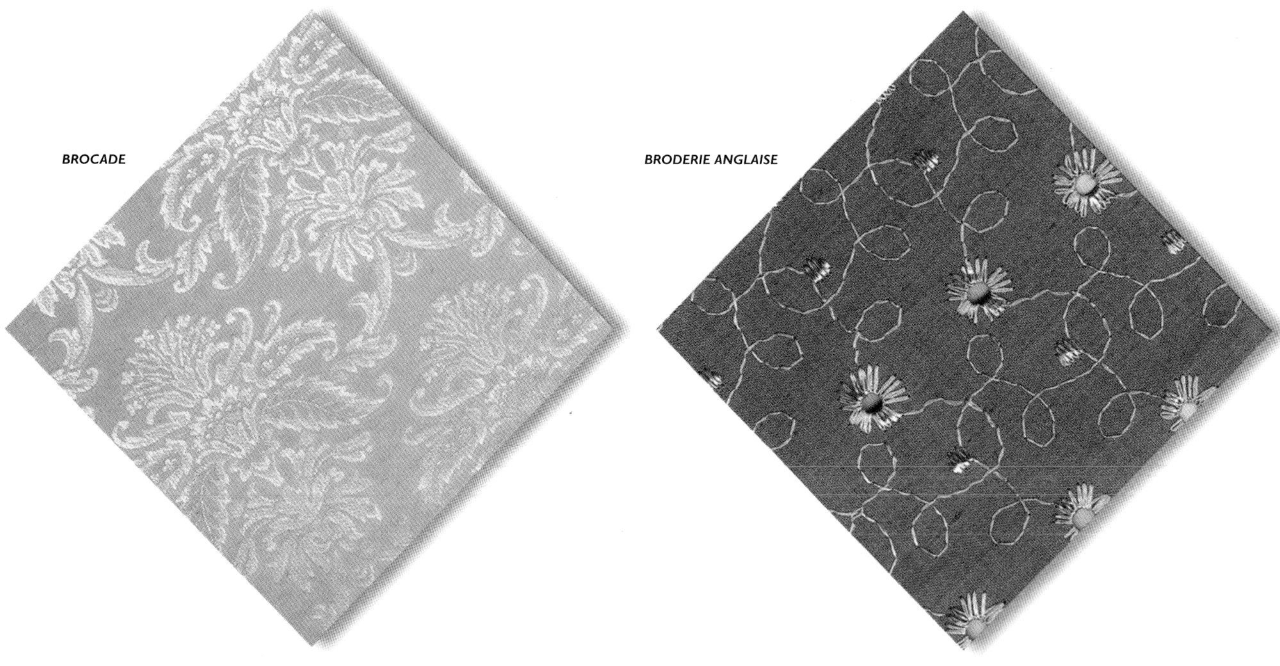

BROCADE

BRODERIE ANGLAISE

### Canvas
A strong, coarse fabric made of cotton or linen, used for awnings and garden chair covers. Use for simple designs because it is heavy to handle. Fasten with metal studs or eyelets threaded with cord.

### Chenille
Fringed yarns are woven to create the soft pile of chenille fabric, which is made of cotton or cotton and man-made-fiber blends. Use chenille to make cushions, bedcovers, and loose covers. The pile will wear and flatten with heavy use.

### Chintz
Chintz is usually printed with pretty, floral designs. It is a fine, closely woven cotton fabric that is widely used for curtains because it drapes well. Plain chintz is very versatile, and is recommended for lining fabrics when the lining needs to be of a good quality because it will be visible, on a bed canopy for example. Glazed chintz has a resin finish, making it resistant to dust and dirt. Dry-clean glazed chintz to preserve its finish.

### Crewelwork
Wool embroidery is worked on thick cotton fabric, traditionally in designs of flowers, trees, and birds. This fabric suits curtains and cushions in an ethnic-style environment.

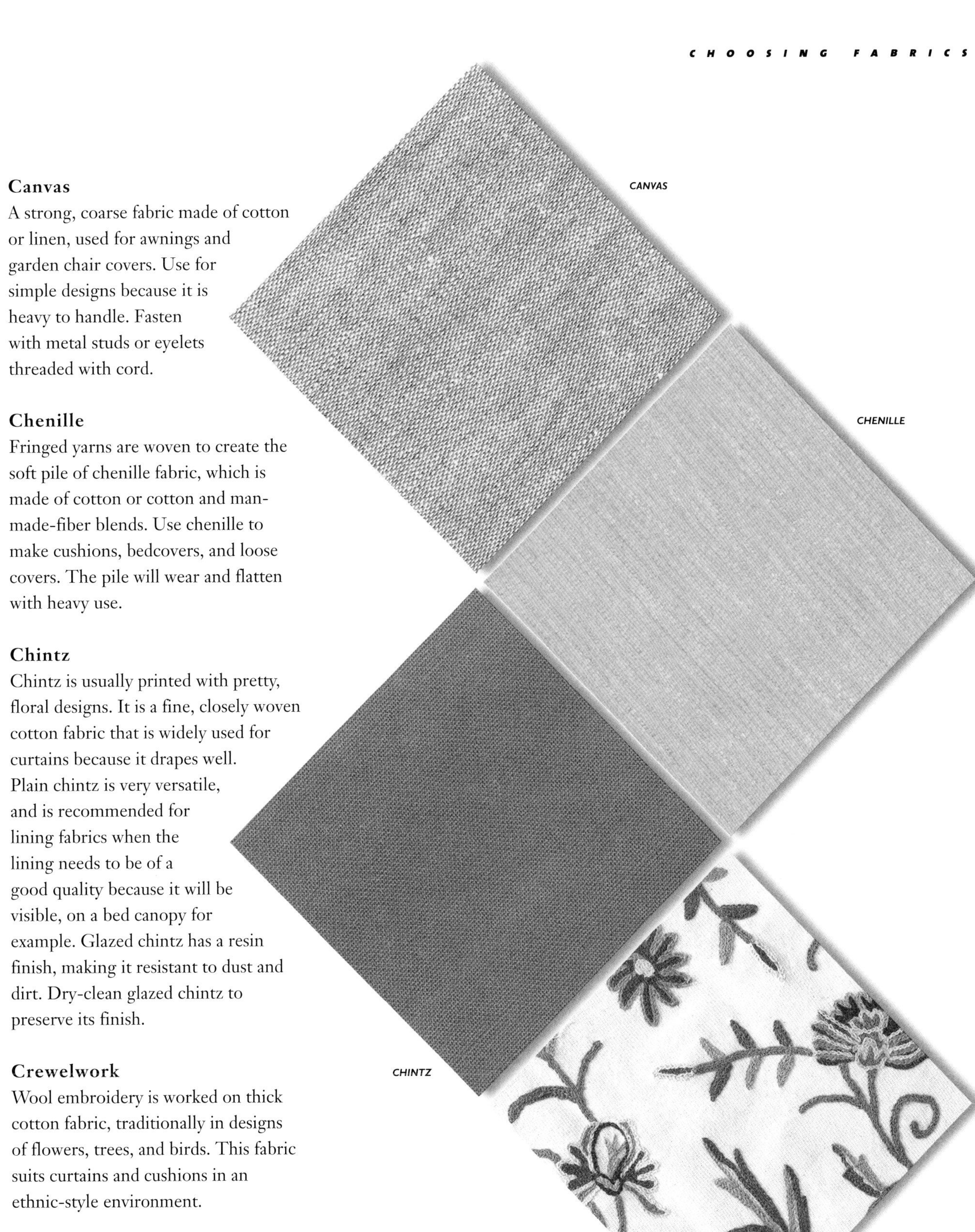
CANVAS

CHENILLE

CHINTZ

CREWELWORK

***When choosing your fabrics you need to be aware of their practical qualities as well as their esthetic appeal. Don't rush the decision: take your time to insure you make the best choice.***

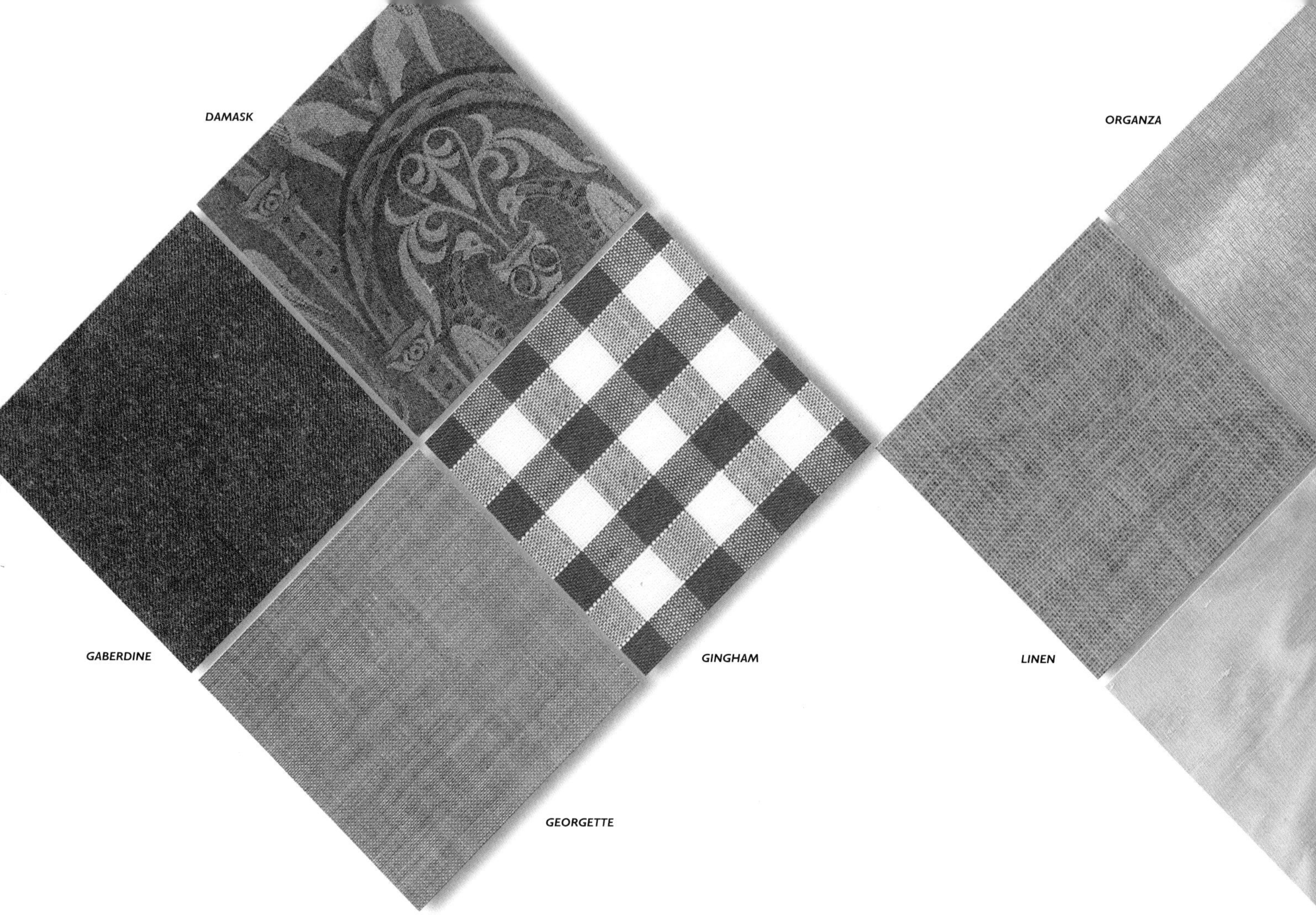


**Damask**

Damask, a very popular choice for soft furnishings, originates from fourteenth-century Damascus. The woven surface designs usually feature flowers, fruits, or figures, and are mostly self-toned, meaning that the design is the same color as the background. Linen damask is traditionally used for tablecloths because it is very elegant but also hard-wearing, and can be boiled and starched to get rid of any stains. When calculating fabric quantities, bear in mind that damask designs are usually one-way.

**Gabardine**

A hard-wearing, closely woven, ribbed fabric made of cotton or wool, and sometimes man-made fibers. Use gabardine for upholstery.

**Georgette**

This fine, floaty fabric is made in a variety of fibers. It does not crease easily and can be used to make sheer curtains and soft blinds. It frays easily, so make double hems, and neaten any seams.

**Gingham**

This colorful and hard-wearing fabric is reminiscent of schooldays. Gingham is usually white with woven checks and sometimes stripes of another color. It is a classic fabric for soft furnishings in children's rooms, for kitchen curtains, and tablecloths.

**Linen**

This strong, natural fabric is available in different weights. It is expensive and creases very easily, but drapes well and feels luxurious. It can be blended with polyester, which makes it easier to handle but of poorer quality. Linen is machine-washable. While damp, press it on the wrong side with a hot iron.

**Organza**

This stiff, lightweight fabric is made from silk, polyester, or viscose. Metallic and hand-painted organzas can be used for dramatic effects. It creases easily, and the creases are difficult to remove. Use organza for sheer curtains, or lay it over another fabric and treat as one to make cushion covers.

**PVC**

PVC is a thermoplastic material. Most fabrics called PVC are knitted or woven cotton that has been sprayed with polyvinyl chloride, making them water-resistant. PVC is firm to handle, does

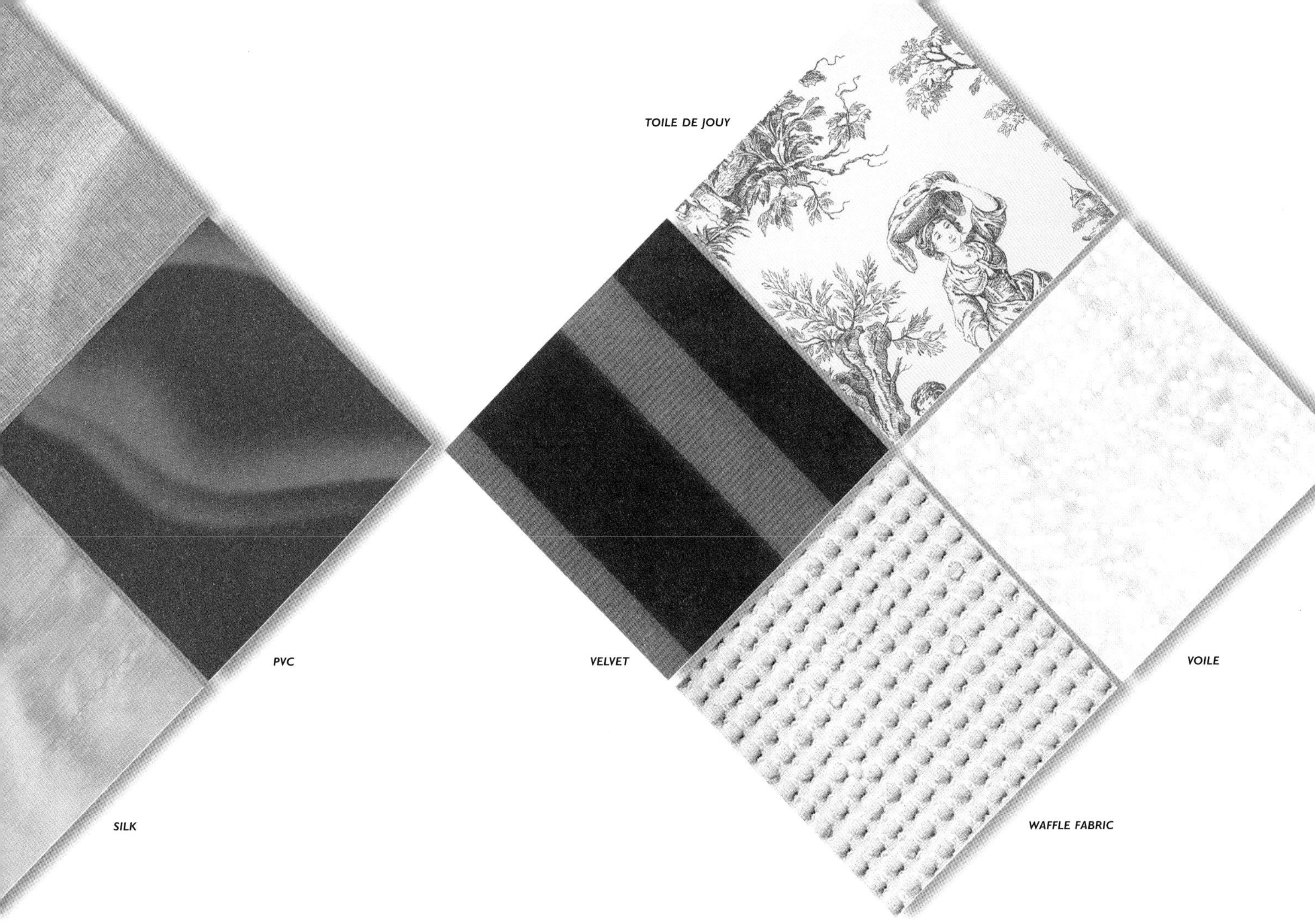


not fray and can be used for simple blinds, tablecloths, and outdoor furnishings. To clean, wipe over with a damp cloth.

### Silk
Silk will bring a touch of glamor and luxury to a room. It is not a hard-wearing fabric, so use it decoratively rather than for items in regular use. It drapes well, but colors fade quickly in sunlight.

### Toile de Jouy
Although this fabric originated in India, it has been made for the last two centuries in Jouy, France. Pastoral engraved designs are printed in one color on natural-colored cottons. This is one of the few designs that works well when used entirely in a room, as a wallcovering, curtains and upholstery, or bed-linen.

### Velvet
Velvet is available in a superb range of rich and luxurious colors, and has a wonderful pile that must always be used in the same direction. This fabric is difficult to handle when making soft furnishings, and should not be tackled by a beginner. If possible, baste and stitch all seams in the direction of the pile. If the fabric puckers, slip tissue paper between the layers. Acrylic velvet, rather than a dressmaking velvet, is recommended for soft furnishings, especially for upholstery because it is harder-wearing and resistant to fading in sunlight. Never wash or spot-clean velvet, instead hang it on a rail and steam-clean it instead. Do not fold velvet or hang it on a clothes hanger, because this will create creases and break the pile; roll it instead.

***Choose the best quality fabric you can afford. Try out a sample of your chosen fabric to make sure that it is suitable for the job. The most up-to-date fabrics will date quickly, so consider buying them only for smaller items.***

### Voile
Made from cotton, man-made fibers, and sometimes silk, voile is a soft, fine fabric used for sheer curtains and soft blinds. Cotton voile can be starched to add body.

### Waffle fabric
The threads in waffle or honeycomb fabric form ridges and valleys on both sides of the cloth, making it very absorbent. It is therefore a practical choice for soft furnishings that will be used in the bathroom or kitchen.

# utility fabrics

A utility fabric has a functional purpose, but many of these fabrics are handsome enough to be used as attractive fabrics in their own right. Hardwearing canvas and ticking come in many bright colorways. They can be used to make cushions and curtains, and can cover items of furniture as well.

### Brushed cotton

A soft, warm, cotton fabric with a slightly fluffy, brushed surface. It is used to interline curtains.

### Buckram

Cotton cloth that is made firm with size to stiffen pleats on curtain headings. It is available in strips or by the yard/meter.

### Bump

A mediumweight interlining for curtains, pelmets, and bedcovers, bump is a thick, fluffy, cotton fabric.

### Burlap

Usually a coarse, loosely woven, jute fabric used for upholstery. It is available in finer weaves and can be used for sturdy curtains, blinds, and wallhangings. Burlap frays easily. Dampen it to pull into shape, because the grain can become distorted.

### Calico

This inexpensive, all-purpose, cotton fabric was first produced in Calcutta, its namesake. Calico is closely woven and available in various weights and widths. It washes and wears well, but does tend to crease easily. Unbleached calico is cream-colored with occasional dark

flecks. For practical purposes, use calico for undercovers and mattress covers—it is very hardwearing, but it can also be used for any soft-furnishing purpose. It has become very popular nowadays because it harmonizes well with other fabrics, dyes efficiently, and is very cheap to buy.

### Cotton sateen

This is a cotton fabric woven with a satin weave, making it very smooth to the touch and with a pleasant sheen. Because it comes in wide widths, cotton sateen is often used to both line curtains and make curtains. Allow extra fabric for shrinkage.

### Domett

A soft and fluffy, open-weave fabric made of wool, or wool and cotton, and used to interline lightweight curtains and bedcovers.

### Interfacing

Use interfacing to stiffen curtain headings, pelmets, and tiebacks. There are woven and non-woven varieties in different weights to match your fabric. They are sold in packs or by the yard/meter, 32¼in/820mm wide. Press-on (fusible) interfacing is pressed to the wrong side of the fabric with an iron.

### Muslin

Use a piece of natural-colored muslin as a pressing cloth. Muslin is also a popular choice for sheer curtains because it is cheap to buy and drapes well, so it can be used in volume.

### Self-adhesive stiffening

This is a self-adhesive card that is cut to shape for pelmets, tiebacks, and lampshades. Its backing is then peeled off to reveal its adhesive surface, which is stuck to the fabric.

### Ticking

This strong fabric is traditionally used for mattress and pillowcovers because its close weave makes it featherproof. Its distinctive, colored stripes on a white background are very striking, making it a popular fabric for soft-furnishing purposes.

### Wadding

Place wadding between fabrics to pad them for making quilts. Cotton wadding is sandwiched between two layers of papery fabric. Polyester wadding is more commonly used; it is much springier than cotton wadding and comes in different weights, such as 2oz/56g, 4oz/113g, and 8oz/226g per yard/meter.

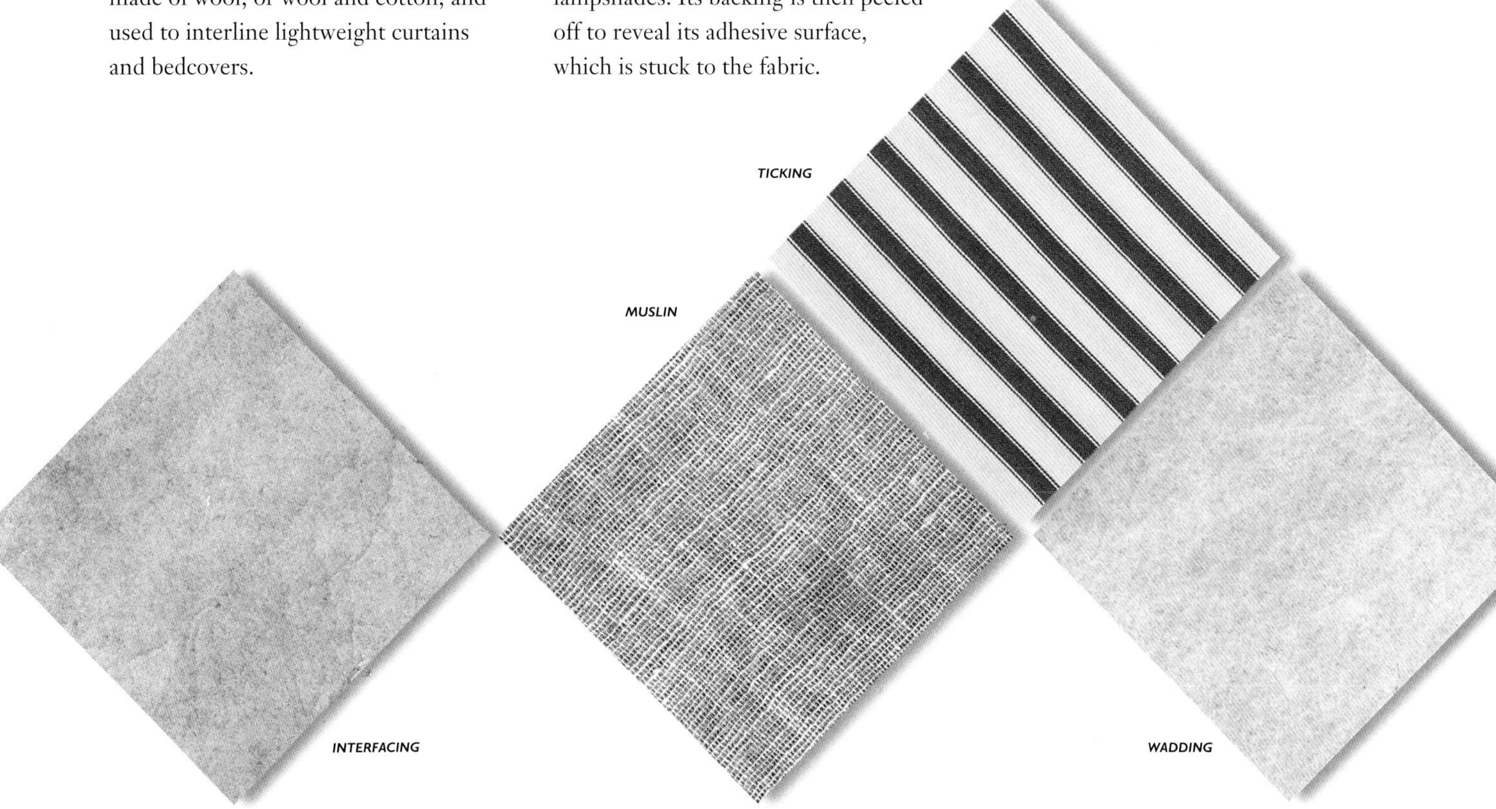
TICKING

MUSLIN

INTERFACING

WADDING

# equipment

It is vital to have the right equipment when you are contemplating beginning a new soft furnishing project: there is nothing worse than getting part of the way through and discovering that you have to go out to buy something vital! Go through what equipment you do have, and add and replace as necessary from the list below.

Even a newcomer to sewing will probably already have some of the equipment needed. Keep your tools together, and use them only on fabrics and their trimmings, so they do not get dirty or blunted. Work on a clean, flat, and well-lit surface, and keep sharp tools beyond the reach of young children and pets. An area lit by a daylight-simulation bulb is kind to the eye and does not alter the color of fabrics, which other light bulbs can do.

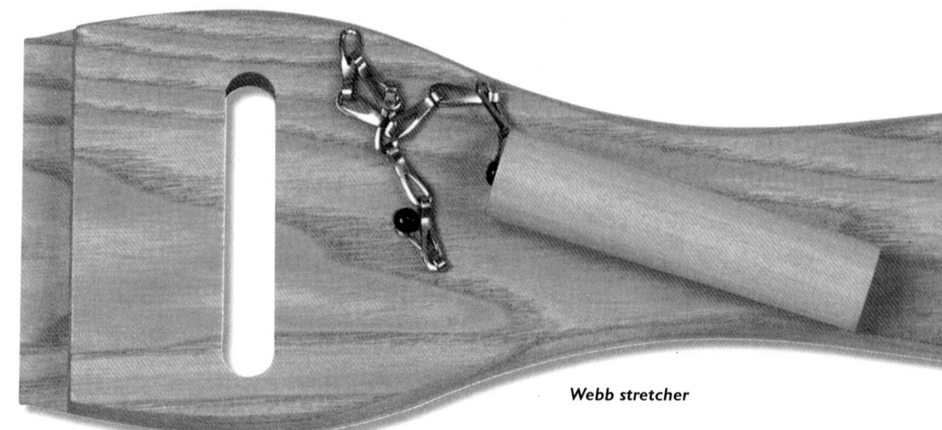

Webb stretcher

### Air-erasable pen

This pen can be used on fabric, because any marks will gradually disappear. Always test on a scrap of fabric first.

### Bias binding maker

This small metal tool is threaded with strips of fabric, which are pulled through and pressed to form bias binding.

Tailor's chalk

### Carpenter's square

Use a carpenter's square for making accurate angles when drawing patterns on paper and fabric.

### Dressmaking shears

Bent-handled dressmaking shears are the most comfortable and accurate to use for cutting fabric—the angle of the lower blade allows the fabric to lay flat. They are available in different lengths, so test the size before buying. A top-quality pair is expensive but will last a lifetime, and it is worth paying that extra bit in the long run.

### Embroidery scissors

A small pair of sharp scissors is indispensable for snipping threads and cutting into intricate areas.

### Hammer

Used to hammer tacks, eyelets, and poppers in place.

### Ironing board and iron

Use a sturdy ironing board—you will find that you will be handling very large and weighty pieces of cloth. Invest in the best iron you can afford, preferably a steam/dry iron with a reliable heat setting.

### Pattern paper

Some patterns can be made directly on to the fabric. However, this lightweight paper is faintly marked with a grid to help with the drawing of patterns. Brown wrapping paper is also suitable.

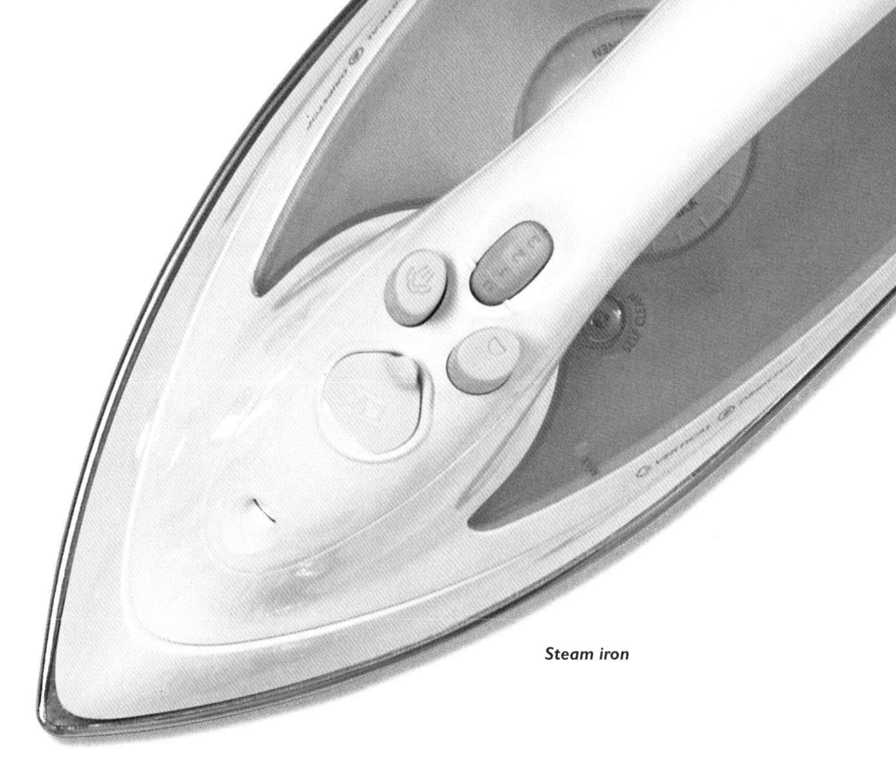
Steam iron

### Pencil
Always keep a propelling pencil or sharp HB pencil and paper to hand in the planning stages. Use a china marker pencil on PVC and vinyl fabrics.

### Pinking shears
These cut a zigzag, fray-resistant edge and are used to neaten seams and cut out fabrics that fray easily.

### Pressing cloth
Use a piece of inexpensive cheesecloth or muslin about 39in/1000mm square to protect the fabric you are pressing from becoming shiny.

### Screwdriver
Use this useful household device to fix screws to walls for curtain tracks, pelmets, and battens for blinds.

### Seam ripper
This small implement has a sharp, inner curve for cutting seams open when mistakes have occurred, and a point for picking out threads.

Pinking shears

### Sewing gauge
This 6in/150mm long rule has a slider that can be set at different levels for marking hems and seams, and as a quilting guide.

### Sewing scissors
One blade is pointed and the other rounded, so fabric can be trimmed without getting snagged.

### Spirit level
Use this to position curtain tracks and battens for blinds.

### Staple gun
This is a fast way of attaching fabric in upholstery, and for fixing swags and tails.

### Steel measure
Use a retractable steel measure to measure windows and beds.

### Tailor's chalk
This colored chalk, available in wedge and pencil forms, is used to mark fabric because it can be brushed off.

### Tape measure
A plastic-coated tape measure is useful for measuring around curves.

### Thimble
A thimble protects your finger when handsewing. Thimbles come in different sizes and are made of leather, metal, or plastic: an open-topped leather thimble is recommended. Wear a thimble on the middle finger.

### Transparent rule
A 12in/305mm rule is a useful size for drawing against on paper and fabric, and for checking measurements.

### Webb stretcher
This is only necessary if you want to do a lot of upholstery. It is used to stretch webbing across the frame of a chair.

### Yard/meter stick
Made from wood or metal, this measure can be used on curtains, and for drawing cutting lines on fabric.

# patterns

Squares and rectangles are the shapes most often cut to make soft furnishings, and these are best marked directly onto the fabric. You will need to make a pattern for shaped items such as tiebacks, lampshades, and seating, specially if you need to cut out more than one piece at a time.

Patterns can be easily made from brown wrapping paper or special pattern-making paper, which is available from soft-furnishing suppliers. Do not use newsprint, because it will dirty the fabric and is too flimsy for the job anyway. Draw the pattern piece on the paper, adding a seam allowance. Mark the grain line, any fold lines, and balance marks such as dots on the seam or notches on the seam allowance; these marks are essential if you are matching one piece of fabric to another. To make a symmetrical pattern piece, fold the paper in half and draw one half of the piece against the fold, then cut out through both layers and open the pattern out flat to use.

If you have made a pattern from fabric—to re-cover a chair, for example—press it flat and mark the seam lines. If you have a set of old loose covers that you wish to use as patterns, check the fit on the piece of furniture in question, and make any alterations that are necessary. Carefully undo all the seams, marking balance marks as you part the pieces. Label the pieces clearly, and mark the top, bottom, and side edges so you know what goes where when you put them on the sofa. Roughly repair any rips, or sew patches over large worn holes so the pattern keeps its shape. Press the patterns flat.

### *Layouts*

Carefully work out how much fabric to buy and the most economical way to arrange the pattern pieces on the paper. Cut down on wastage as much as you can. Bear in mind whether the fabric has a nap—this means a pile that runs in one direction, or a design that works in one direction only, in which case the patterns need to lay in the same direction. Allow extra for matching patterned fabrics (see page 21).

Use the width of the fabric to calculate how much fabric to buy. If most of the pieces are to be cut from measurements, i.e. squares or rectangles, take a sheet of paper to represent the fabric, the side edges being the selvages. Draw the pieces on the paper, marking their dimensions and adding them up so they fit across the width. Mark on their dimensions and grain lines, and butt the edges together to lessen wastage. Check that seam allowances and hems are included. Next, add the dimensions along the side "selvage" edges to the amount of fabric. Keep the layout diagram for positioning when cutting.

For shaped pattern pieces, use long rules and tape measures on a large table or the floor to mark out an area that is the width of the fabric, or half the width of the fabric if you need to cut patterns in pairs. Arrange the patterns within the space, keeping grain lines level with the marked edges that represent the selvages or a selvage and fold. If the fabric has a nap, make sure all the pieces lay in the correct direction. Check that you have included all pattern pieces, as some may need to be repeated. The length of the table or floor area taken up by the patterns is the length of fabric needed. Make a rough sketch of the layout to refer to when positioning for cutting.

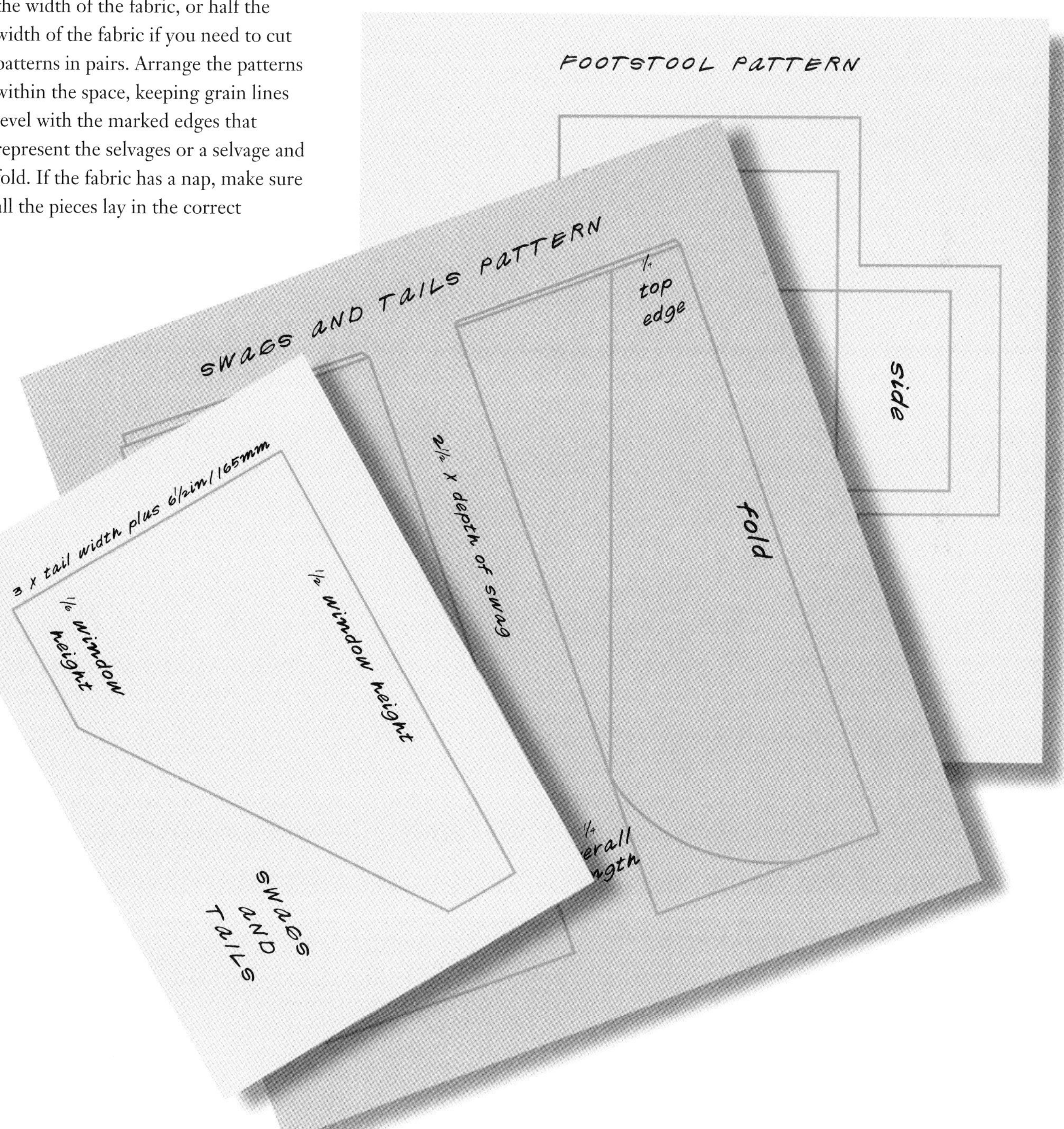


***Draw the pattern on your piece of paper, marking the seams and any fold lines. Also of importance are the direction of the grain and balance marks on the seam, and seam allowance.***

# cutting out

Cutting out the fabric is a major part of creating soft furnishings. Do not rush this stage—cutting mistakes can be costly, as most cannot be rectified. Though it is tempting to rush right in and get started, take your time to position the pattern pieces correctly and economically—this will save you time later on.

## Cutting selvages

*It is often advisable to cut off selvages (the neatened edges that run the length of the fabric), because they are woven tighter than the fabric, sometimes causing it to pucker. If you join fabric widths with the selvages on, cut into the seam allowances at 4in/100mm intervals to release any tightness.*

*Lay the fabric out flat on a large table or the floor, depending upon the size of the fabric: ideally, the cutting area should be accessible from at least three sides. To cut pairs of patterns, fold the fabric in half lengthwise, or widthwise if that suits your layout better; alternately, keep the fabric single and cut each piece individually.*

## How to cut out

*1 Pin the pattern pieces on top, matching the grain lines, or draw the dimensions of the pieces with an air-erasable pen or tailor's chalk. Use a rule and carpenter's square to draw straight lines and right angles.*

*2 Cut out the pieces, cutting thick fabrics one layer at a time, and patterned fabrics the same so you can match the designs accurately. Save fabric scraps for testing stitches and the heat of the iron.*

*3 On vinyl or leather, stick pattern pieces in place on the wrong side with painter's tape, and draw around the piece with an air-erasable pen or tailor's chalk. Remove the pattern, and cut out the fabric one layer at a time.*

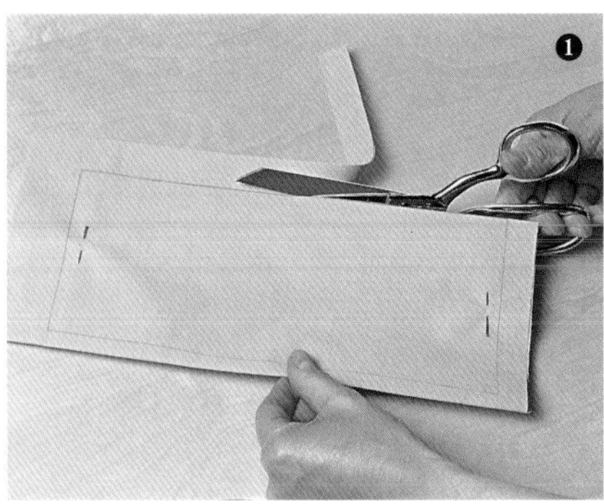

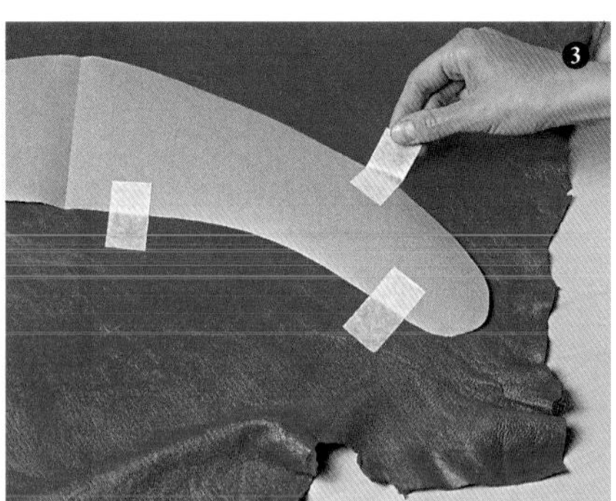

## Matching patterned fabrics

1 Use an air-erasable pen or tailor's chalk to draw a line across the fabric selvage to selvage. Avoid placing the line through a design motif, because this will disrupt the overall effect. Cut off excess fabric above an upper seam or hem allowance. Lay the fabric out flat, right side up, on a large table or the floor. Measure the length of the curtain including allowances, and cut off the excess fabric.

2 Lay the remaining fabric selvage to selvage with this first piece, matching the level of the pattern. Cut across the fabric to match the first piece. Cut any remaining pieces in the same way. Cut off the selvages.

3 Fold under a ⅝in/15mm seam allowance along one long edge. Lay the folded edge over the adjacent edge of the other length of fabric, matching the pattern. Pin and ladder stitch the pieces together.

4 Now fold over the top fabric so the right sides are together. Stitch the seam, using a flat felled seam for unlined curtains, and a flat seam for lined curtains.

## Matching pattern repeats

*Extra fabric must be allowed for matching patterned fabrics. In general, add one pattern repeat for each fabric width. The pattern repeat is usually marked on the fabric label; if not, ask the retailer to measure the repeat.*

*Widths of fabric usually need to be joined to make curtains, but this is also sometimes necessary when making bedcovers and re-covering sofas.*

*Extra fabric may also be needed for positioning an element of the fabric design to show it whole and at its best, on the center of a cushion, for example. Though this means extra expense, it will give a satisfying end result. Make a pattern from stiff, waxed or tracing paper so you can see through it. Fold it into quarters to find the center, open out flat, and mark the fold lines and grain line. Lay the pattern over a motif on the fabric, matching the grain lines and the center of the pattern to the center of the design. Pin in place and cut out.*

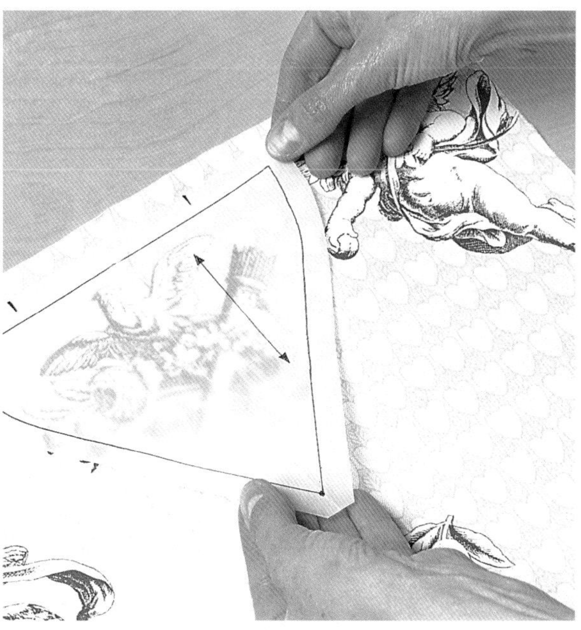

# basic techniques

Many people have more sewing skills than they realize. Tackling a simple soft furnishings project for the home will bring these skills to light. Don't despair if you have never attempted larger projects before—try out anything you are unsure of on scrap pieces of fabric, and take everything slowly.

The same basic methods are repeated throughout this book, so read through this section carefully before embarking on any project. Try out new techniques on scrap fabric first, rather than experiment on the item itself. When following instructions, it is important to use imperial or metric measurements, but not a combination of both.

***Seams*** Before stitching, carefully match the seam allowances and patterns. Position pins at right angles to the seam and stitch over the pins, or place them along the seam line and remove them as you stitch. Experiment and see which method you prefer—it may be a combination of both. If you are a nervous stitcher, or are working on an awkward area, baste the seams together first.

***Flat seam*** This is the simplest seam to stitch. Use a flat seam to join fabric widths for lined curtains, and to join layers that will be bagged out, e.g. cushion covers.

***Flat felled seam*** This is a neat seam that can be used on unlined curtains, and other items where both sides of the fabric will be visible because the raw edges are enclosed.

***French seam*** This seam is best suited to lightweight fabrics, see-through fabrics (where you don't want a bulky seam showing through), and ones that tend to fray easily. The raw edges are enclosed within the seam, giving a neat finish, and stopping loose fibers escaping to spoil the item.

***Layering seam allowances*** When you have many seam allowances together, it is best to layer them to reduce their bulk. Consult the box below for instructions.

***Clipping corners and curves*** To reduce bulk at stitched corners, cut diagonally across the seam allowance at the corner.

***Neatening seams*** To prevent fraying, neaten flat seams with a zigzag stitch or pinking shears.

***Topstitching*** Topstitching is worked on the right side of the fabric for both functional and decorative purposes. Topstitching is applied after the item has been stitched together.

## Making a flat seam

*With right sides facing, stitch fabric layers together along the seam line.*

## Layering a seam

*To reduce the bulk of thick fabrics in flat seams or seams of many layers, e.g. piped seams, trim each seam allowance to a different amount.*

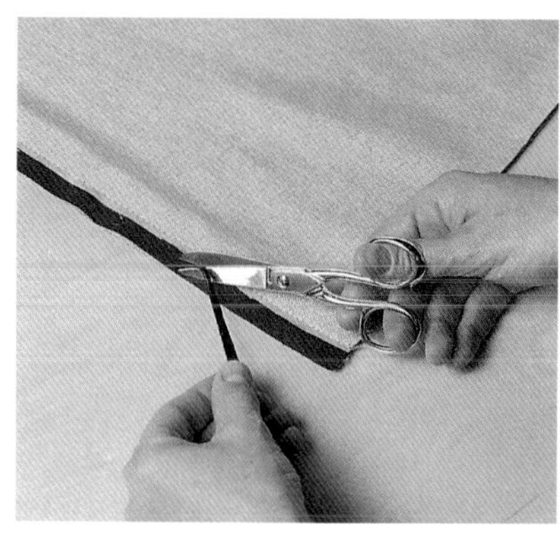

## Making a flat felled seam

1 With right sides facing, stitch a flat seam, taking a ⅝in/15mm allowance. Press the seam allowances in the same direction, then trim the lower seam allowance to ⅜in/10mm.

2 Turn under ¼in/6mm on the upper seam allowance. Stitch close to the turned-under edge.

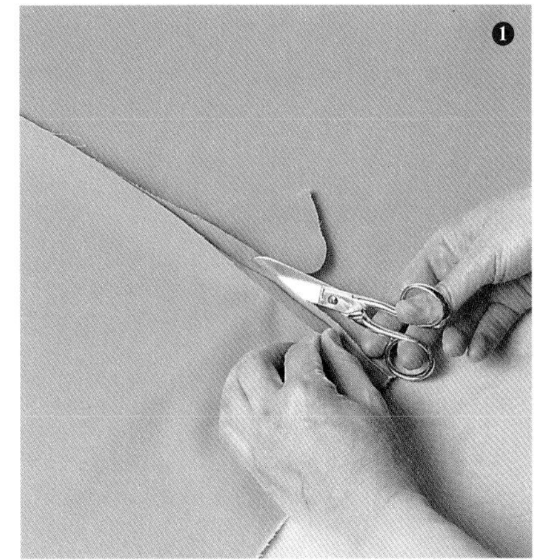

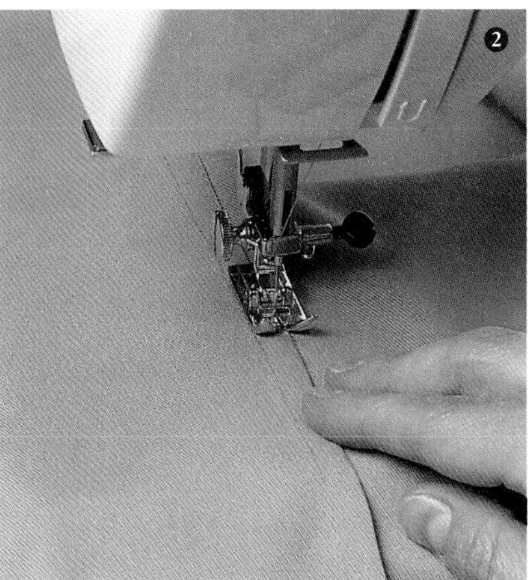

## Making a French seam

1 Stitch a flat seam with wrong sides facing, taking a 5/16in/7.5mm seam allowance. Trim seam allowances to ¼in/6mm.

2 Turn fabric with right sides facing, and stitch 5/16in/7.5mm from the first seam.

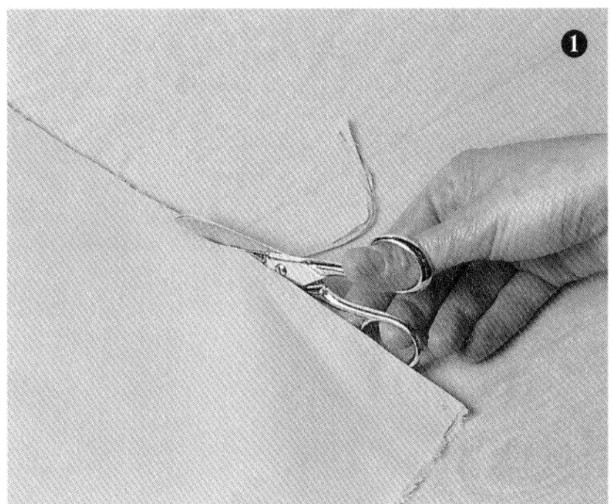

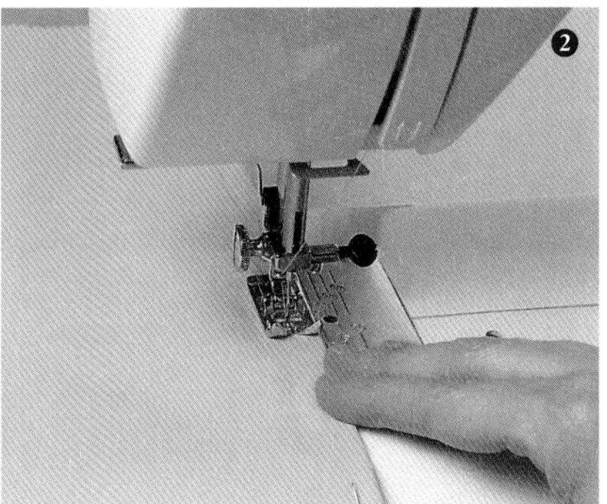

## Clipping corners and curves

*Snip into curved seam allowances. This will help the fabric lay flat on corners and more undulating shapes. Remember not to cut too close to the stitching of the seam.*

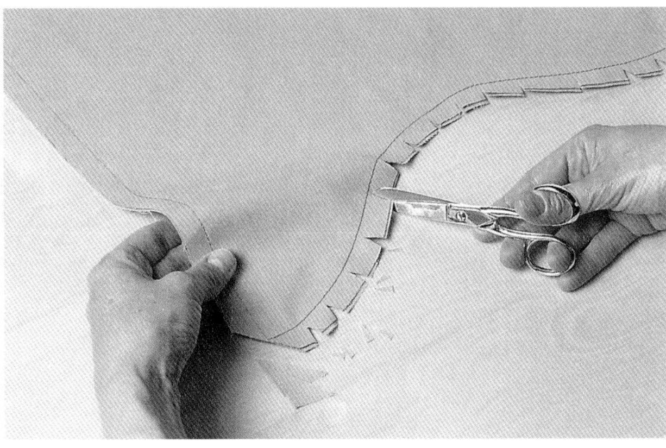

## Topstitching

*Stitch parallel to a seam to emphasize it, and to hold the seam allowance in place. Contrasting, colored or thick machine sewing thread will accentuate the stitching.*

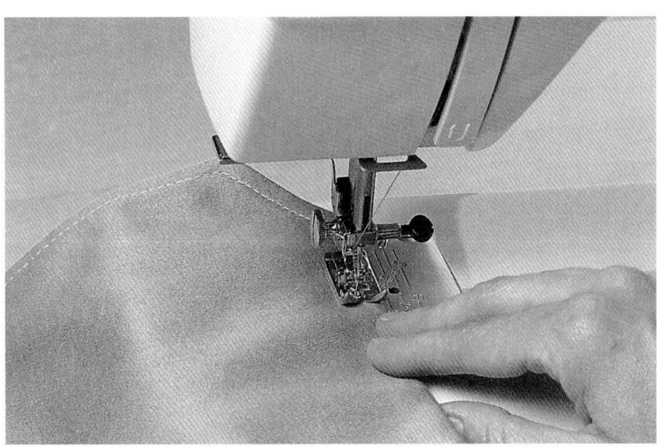

### *Hand stitches*

Hand stitching is an essential part of any sewing process, and soft furnishing projects are no exception. Some fabrics lend themselves to being hemmed by hand, for example, and basting is vital.

***Basting*** The more you stitch, the more confident you will become, and therefore less reliant on needing to baste before stitching. (However, it is always a good idea to do so.) Basting is useful for tricky areas or joining many layers of fabric, however. Work the basting stitches in a contrasting, colored thread so they are easy to see when you come to remove them later. Basting thread comes in a limited range of colors, but any sewing thread will do.

***Slipstitch*** Slipstitching is used to join two folded edges or one folded edge to a flat surface, such as to close openings in seams, to secure bindings in place, or to hem light to mediumweight fabric. The stitches should be almost invisible. Working from right to left, bring the needle out through one folded edge. Pick up a few threads of the adjoining fabric, and then a few threads on the folded edge. Repeat along the length.

***Herringbone stitch*** Herringbone stitch is used to hem heavyweight fabrics, and to join the butted edges of wadding together. The stitches are worked from left to right, with the needle pointing to the left. Bring the needle to the right side.

***Finger-pressing*** It is not always possible to get the tip of the iron into intricate corners to press the seam. (See the text below for more details.)

***Cord tidy*** Cords on curtain tapes should not be cut off once the heading has been drawn up. Make a small bag to slip the excess cord into, to allow the heading to be opened out flat again, for laundering or hanging at a different-size window.

***Temporary basting*** This is a practical way of fixing fabric to a solid frame whilst working. Even if you intend to staple the fabric with a staple gun, in many instances it is helpful to use temporary basting first.

## How to baste

*Pin the layers together, then work a long running stitch by hand. Set the machine to a long stitch length for basting by machine.*

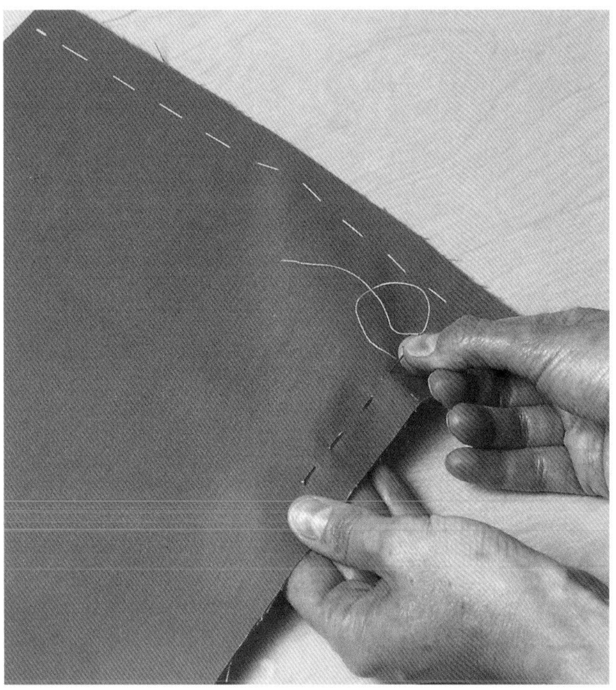

## How to finger-press

*If you can't reach the seam with the iron, simply moisten your finger and run it along the seam to finger-press.*

## Making a cord tidy

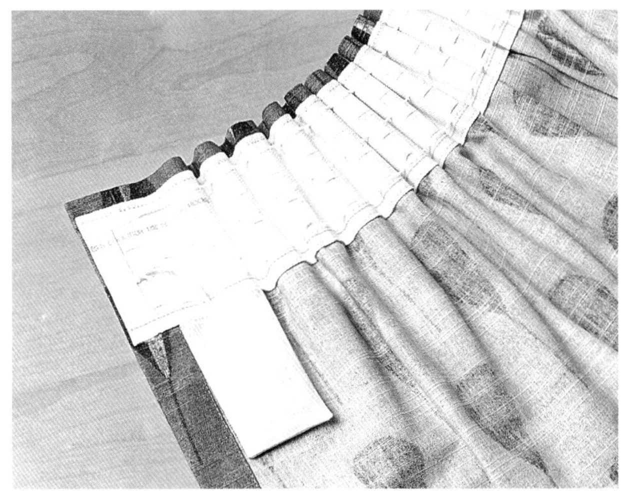

1 *Cut a rectangle of fabric such as calico 4¾ x 4in/120 x 100mm. Fold widthwise in half, with the right sides facing. Stitch the raw edges, taking a ⅜in/10mm seam allowance and leaving a 1¼in/32mm gap in the short upper edge.*

2 *Clip the corners and turn right side out. Slip the cords into the bag, and sew it to the top of the curtain on the underside.*

## How to herringbone stitch

1 *Make the first small stitch through the fabric above and ¼–⅜in/6–10mm to the right.*

2 *Make the next stitch below and ¼–⅜in/6–10mm to the right. Continue to alternate stitches and space them evenly apart.*

## Temporary tacking

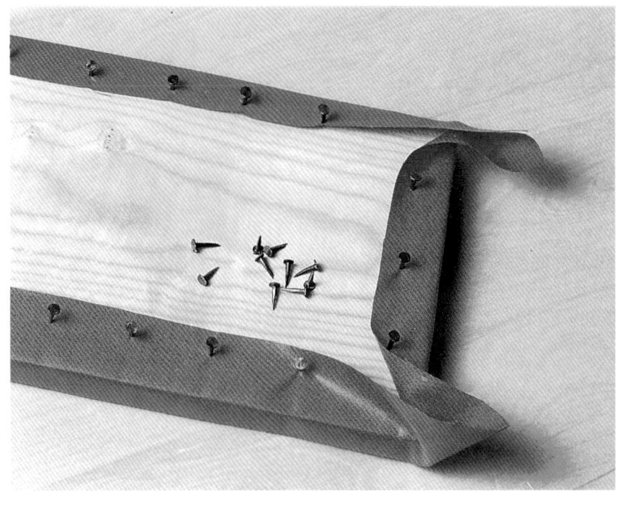

1 *Lever off old tacks with a tack lifter, which is a traditional upholstery tool, or use the blade of a screwdriver. If the head snaps off a tack, hammer the shaft into the wood to prevent it snagging the fabric.*

2 *Drive the tack halfway home with a hammer—it is then easy to remove for repositioning. A tack hammer with a magnetic tip will hold a tack in place. Hammer the tack in straight; if it starts to lay crooked, remove it and start again, or knock it upright. If it does not lay straight, the head may snag the fabric and you.*

### *Bindings*

Curved raw edges should be bound with bias-cut binding. The binding can be manipulated to follow the contours of the fabric, but will still lie flat. This is because the bias grain is the stretchiest part of the fabric.

***Cutting bias strips*** Though ready-made bias binding is inexpensive and widely available, it is very economical to make your own, and it has many uses, such as binding raw edges, covering piping, and making ties. When working out what the width of the strips should be, use a tape measure to measure around the front and back of the fabric edge to be bound. Generally, cut strips for bias binding are double the finished width, to allow for seam allowances and stretching. The seam allowance should match that of the item when cutting strips to make piping.

***Joining bias strips*** Once cut, bias strips can be easily joined and then sewn together securely with the machine. (See the text opposite for more details.)

***Making bias binding*** A bias binding maker is very useful for making single bias binding, and you will find the whole process very satisfying. This handy gadget is available in most soft-furnishing departments and stores. (See text opposite for using one.)

Some fabrics are easier to handle double when applying a binding. Make sheer fabric bindings double. A bias binding maker is not needed to make a double binding. Simply press the strip lengthwise in half with the right sides facing.

***Attaching double bias binding*** Double bias binding is useful when you are working with sheer or lightweight fabrics. (See text opposite for how to attach double bias binding.)

## Cutting bias strips

1 *Measure the length of the edge that is to be bound, adding 4in/100mm for ease and turning under the ends. Extra will need to be added for joining lengths.*

2 *Fold fabric diagonally, at a 45-degree angle to the selvage. This diagonal fold is the true bias. Press along the fold, then open out flat. With tailor's chalk or an air-erasable pen and rule, draw lines the width of the binding that are parallel with the fold line. Cut out along these lines.*

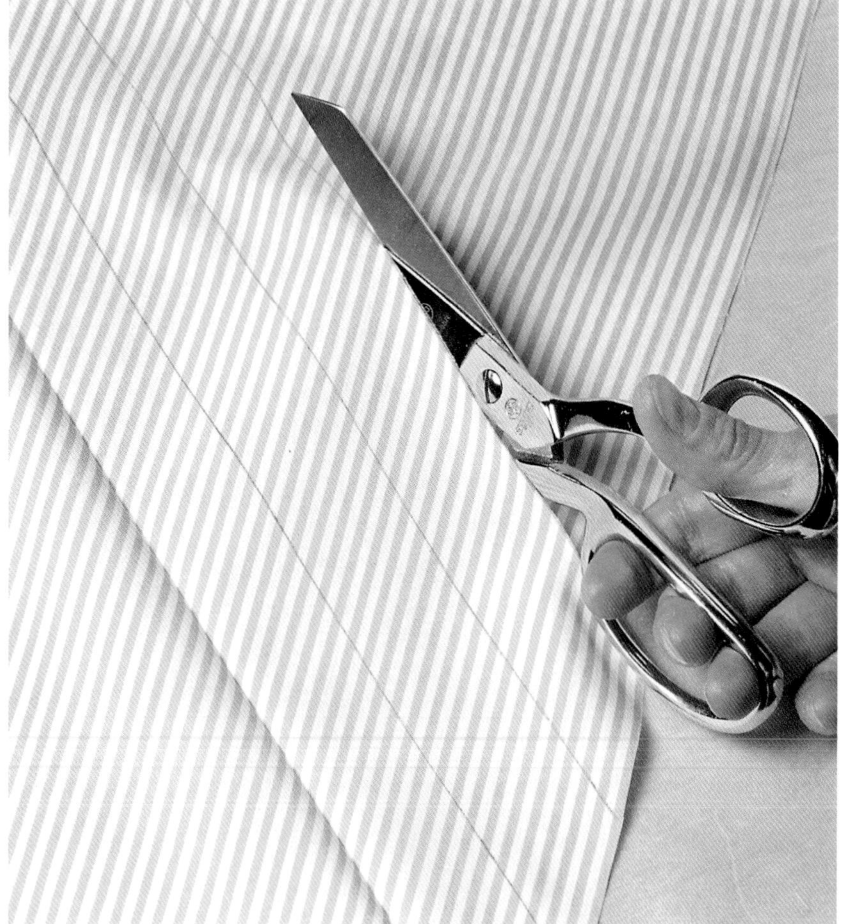

## Attaching single bias binding

1 *Open out one folded edge of the bias binding. With right sides facing and matching the raw edges, pin the binding to the fabric. Stitch along the fold line.*

2 *Turn the binding to the underside, and slipstitch the fold along the seam line.*

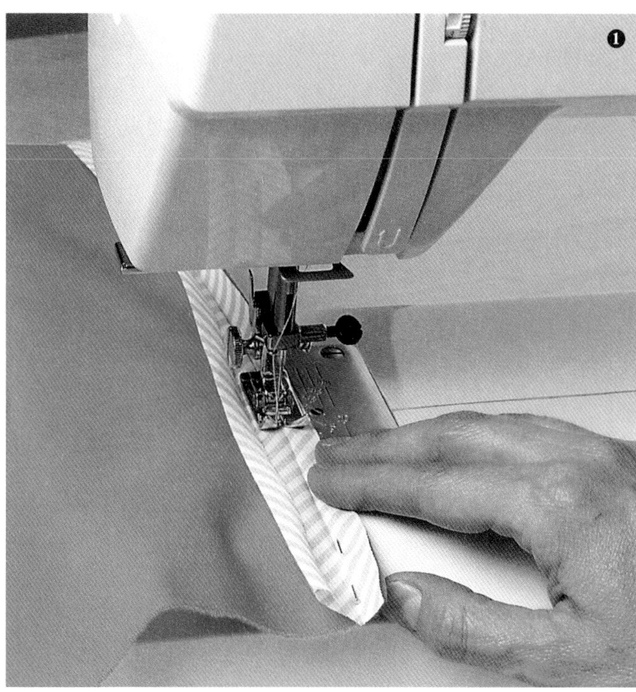

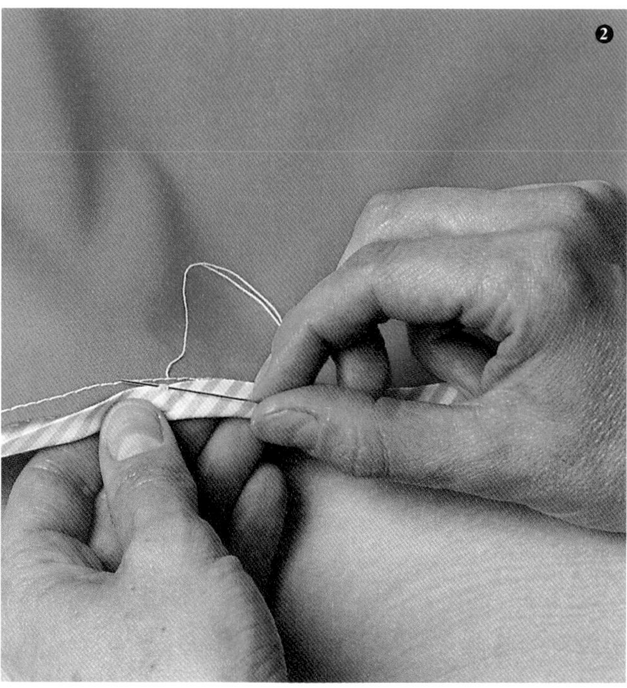

## Joining bias strips

*Position one end of two strips at right angles to each other, with the right sides facing and the raw ends matched. Stitch the bias strips together, taking a ¼in/6mm seam allowance. Press the seam open, then cut off the corners.*

## Making bias binding

*Push the strip through the wide end of the binding maker, with the wrong side of the fabric face up. If the fabric is thick, a pin is useful to ease it out of the narrow end. As the strip emerges through the narrow end, the edges will be turned under. Press them in place.*

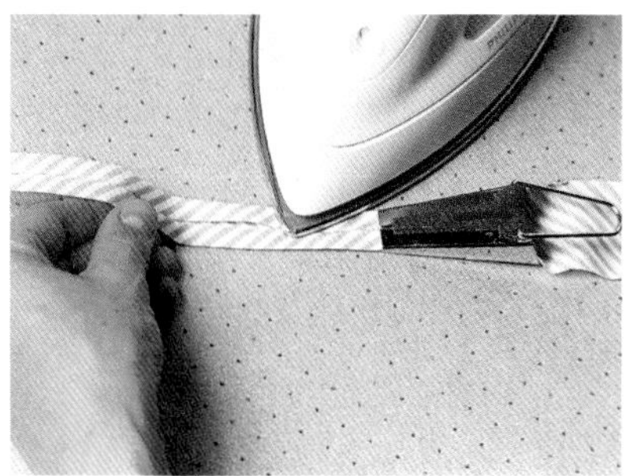

## Attaching double bias binding

*Pin the double bias binding on the right side of the fabric, matching the raw edges. Stitch the bias binding in place, then turn the folded edge to the underside and slipstitch along the seam.*

*Piping*
Piping gives a nicely finished look to many handsewn items, from the edges of cushions to lampshades and throws. You can buy quite a wide range of different kinds of piping in soft-furnishing stores, but it is very easy to make your own. Then you can be sure that you will get your piping either to match or contrast with the fabric of your finished item.

***Making piping*** Although piping is available ready made by the yard/meter, the color range is limited. Make your own piping by covering piping cord, which comes in various thicknesses. Wash it first to preshrink.

***Applying piping and turning corners*** Piping should be basted into place and then machine stitched. Turning corners can be daunting, but it is just a question of taking it slowly. (See text opposite for more details.)

***Joining the piping ends*** Piping cord can be slightly frustrating, because it can fray amazingly easily. Joining it smoothly is easier than you think, and always leaves a very pleasing (and hopefully invisible!) result. (See text opposite for more details.)

***Stitching piping*** Lay the second piece of fabric on top of the basted piped fabric with right sides facing. Baste through all the layers. With a zipper or piping foot on the sewing machine, stitch the piping in position.

***Attaching cord*** If cord is to be sewn along a seam, leave a 1¼in/32mm gap in the seam in an unobtrusive place, such as the lower edge of a cushion, or carefully cut a gap in a stitched seam.

## Making piping

1 *Measure the circumference of the cord and add a 1¼in/32mm seam allowance—this is the width of the bias strip needed to cover the cord. Cut a bias strip of fabric in this width and to the length needed. Join bias strips if necessary. When measuring an item to calculate how much piping is needed, add 4in/100mm for ease and joining ends.*

2 *Lay the cord along the center of the strip on the wrong side. Fold the strip lengthwise in half, enclosing the cord. Pin the raw edges together. Set the sewing machine to a long length stitch for machine basting. Using a zipper or piping foot, stitch close to the piping.*

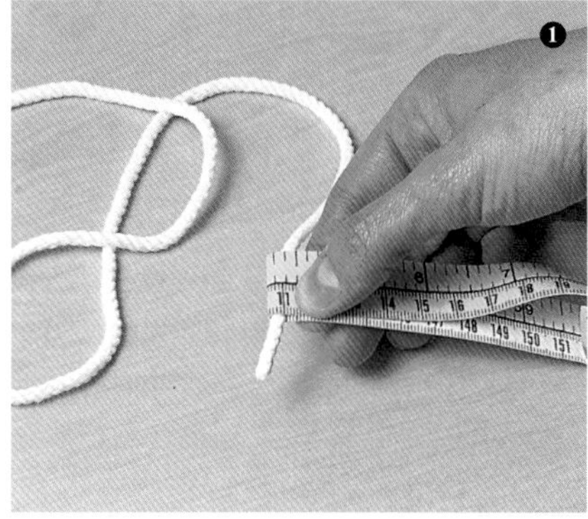
1

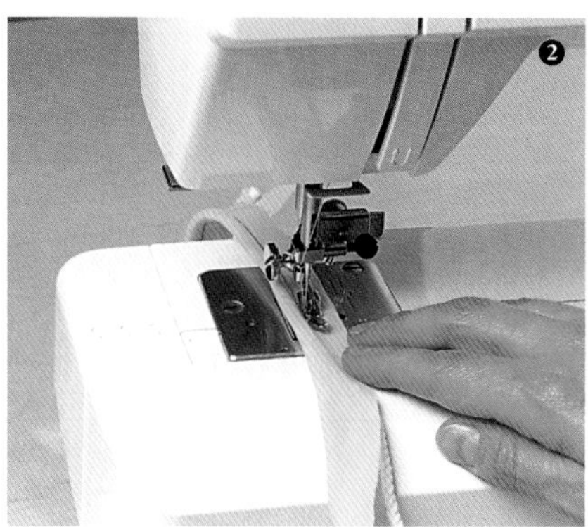
2

## Joining the piping ends

1 *To join the ends of the piping neatly, allow a 1in/25mm overlap and pin the piping in place to 2in/50mm each side of the overlap. Unpick the piping basting for 2in/50mm each side of the overlap to reveal the cord. Cut off half the strands at each end of the cord to thin it.*

2 *Twist the ends of the cord together and bind with thread. Wrap one end of the piping fabric around the cord again. Turn under ¼in/6mm on the other end and wrap it around the cord. Baste the cord in place ready for stitching.*

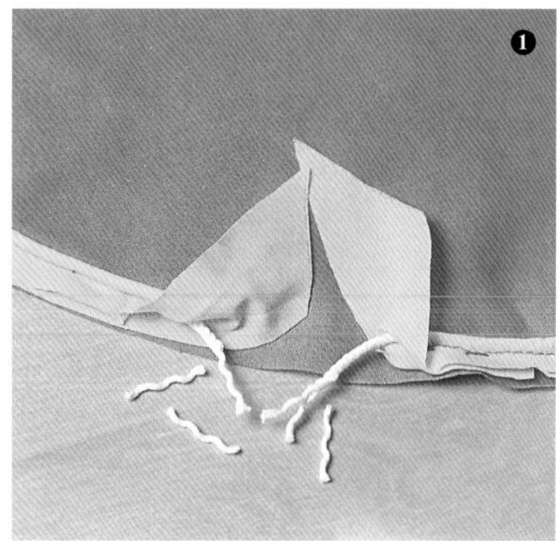
1

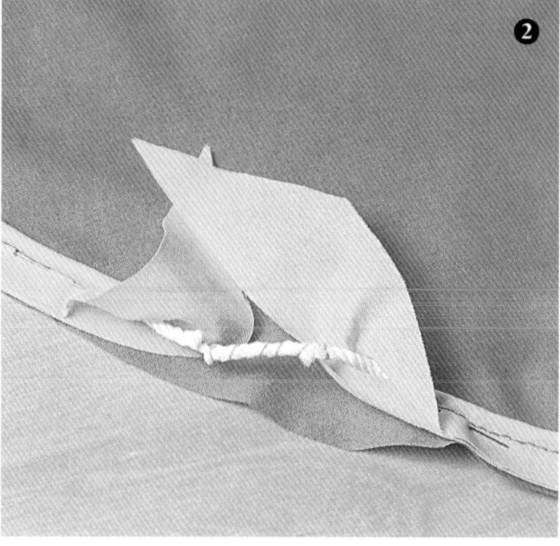
2

## Applying piping and turning corners

*Pin the piping to the right side of the fabric. Snip the seam allowance of the piping at curves and corners. Baste in place by hand or machine, using a zipper or piping foot.*

### *Mounting fabric*

There are many beautiful sheer fabrics available today, and it may often seem that their application is rather limited because they are quite delicate and slippery. Sheer or unstable fabrics can be mounted onto denser fabrics, however, to give them some stability, then the two fabrics can be treated as one. This technique is not suitable for large areas of fabric or areas prone to lots of wear, but it is ideal for smaller cushion covers and table runners. Consider the color of the underlaying fabric carefully, because it will be visible and will be affected by the color or loose weave of the fabric on top.

***Bonding web*** Bonding web is a fusible webbing used to apply fabric to fabric. It is ideal for appliqué work. It is simply pressed on.

## How to mount fabric

*Pin the sheer fabric to a background fabric, starting at the center, and smoothing the layers outward. Baste the fabrics together along the outer edges.*

## Attaching cord

*Unravel one end of the cord so it is not so bulky, and poke it into the hole. Lay the cord along the seam and catch it in place with small stitches. Unravel the other end and poke it into the hole, sewing the gap closed securely.*

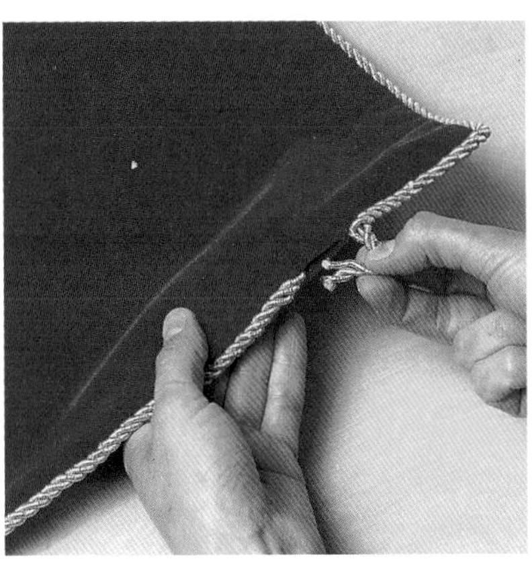

## Applying bonding web

1 *Draw your design on the paper backing side of the bonding web. Be aware that a mirror image of the design should be drawn. Roughly cut out the shape and press it onto the wrong side of the fabric.*

2 *Cut out the design. Peel off the backing paper and position it right side up on the background fabric. Press the motif to fuse it in place.*

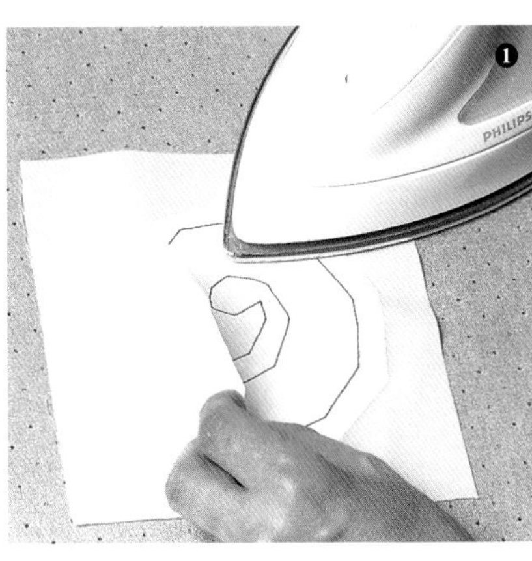


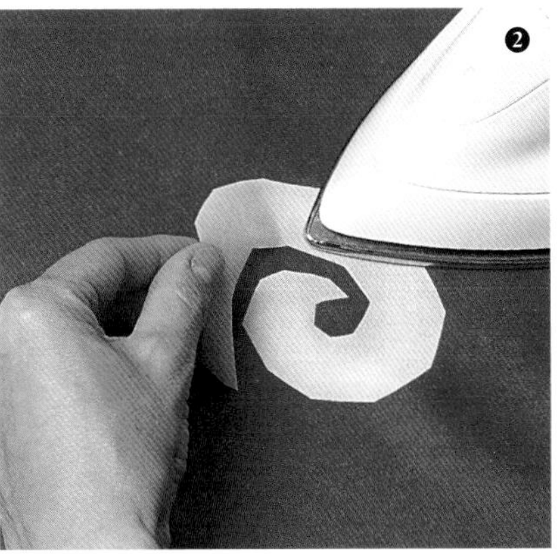

# windows

Making curtains may seem like a difficult task, but provided you have taken the measurements carefully, chosen the right fabric, and you follow the techniques shown on the following pages, you'll be able to accent your windows with the most wonderful arrangements.

Don't jump in at the deep end, but begin by making simple unlined curtains—when you feel confident, progress to more complex types. Then try some, or all, of the projects. You can choose the formality of French pleat curtains and Roman blinds, or the informality of swags and tails. Don't forget, you can always add your own ideas to personalize them still further.

# calculating measurements

Before taking the plunge into making curtains, loose covers, and bed linen, it is vital that you take all the measurements you need. This is a part of the process that must not be rushed—you don't want to spend hours working on a pair of curtains, then find that they are too short when you hang them at your window, for example.

Ideally, have the curtain or blind fittings in place before measuring for fabric. If this is not possible, lightly mark their intended position on the wall or window frame. Slip a few hooks or rings onto the track or pole. To make a window seem larger and to let more light into the room, extend curtain tracks or poles beyond the frame so that curtains can be pulled right back to the edges of the frame.

### *Measuring the length*

For gathered headings on a track and for curtains with casings, measure the length from the top of the track or pole. For tab-top curtains or curtains hanging from rings, measure from the bottom of the tab or ring. For case-headed curtains, measure from below the pole. For blinds, measure from the top of the batten.

Consider what is in front of the window when deciding upon the length of a curtain or blind. If there is furniture in front, a sill-length curtain may be the best option so that the curtain is easy to draw and does not interfere with the furniture. If there is a radiator in front of the window, below-sill-length curtains that finish just above the top of the radiator will allow heat from the radiator to warm the room well when the curtains are closed.

Floor-length curtains can finish just above the floor surface or flow onto the floor for a more elaborate effect; soft fabrics work best for this type of window dressing—if the fabric is thick, it will just pile up unattractively on the floor and look as if the curtains have been made to the wrong length!

Add an allowance for the heading and lower hem to the length. For a standard heading and pencil pleats, add 1½in/38mm to the upper edge. For curtains with a casing, use a cloth tape measure to measure the circumference of the pole, adding ⅜in/10mm for ease plus ¾in/20mm seam allowance; extra will be needed for a frill at the top, so allow twice the height of the frill. Add a ⅝in/15mm seam allowance to the top of tab-top or tie curtains. The depth of the hem will vary according to the fabric, but generally add 6in/150mm for unlined curtains, and 4in/100mm for lined curtains. See individual blind instructions for hems and allowances.

### *Measuring the width*

Measure the width of the track or pole with a steel tape or long wooden rule. For overlapping curtain tracks in two halves, add the length of the overlap.

Multiply this measurement by 1½–3 for a gathered heading, by 2–2½ for pencil-pleated heading, and by 2 for triple- and cylindrical-pleated headings. Add a 1in/25mm hem at each side for unlined curtains, and a 1½in/38mm hem to each side for lined curtains.

### *Fabric widths*

Unless a window is extremely narrow, widths of fabric will need to be be joined together to make curtains. Divide the total width measurement by the width of your chosen fabric for the number of fabric widths required. Round up the fabric widths to the largest amount, because 1¼in/32mm seam allowances are also needed for each join. (See pages 20–21 for pattern repeats and joining widths.) If you have an uneven number of fabric widths and there will be a pair of curtains at the window, cut one width lengthwise in half and place it at the outer edge of the curtains.

### *Lining*

The same amount of lining is needed as for the curtain fabric, but do not allow extra for matching patterns.

***A soft, light fabric can flow onto the floor in a very elegant style. You should avoid using a thick fabric to create this effect.***

# making curtains

Curtains can be daunting to make—especially if you have never made them before. Start with a simple pair of unlined curtains, and work your way up as you get more confident. As long as you have done all your measuring accurately and are using the correct type of fabric for your chosen curtain, it is difficult to go wrong.

### *Unlined curtains*

Unlined curtains are quick and easy to make, but do not hang as well as lined curtains. They are not usually light-fast, so may not be suitable for a bedroom or bathroom. (See page 32 to calculate fabric quantities.) If you want the fabric to stand above the tape, add double the height of the stand to the length measurements. You will also need standard or pencil-pleat tape the entire width of the curtain.

### *Loose-lined curtains*

A detachable lining is very versatile, because it can be removed from the main curtain for laundering. This is useful if the curtain and lining have differing washing instructions. Even if they have the same washing procedure, if a curtain is very bulky it may not fit into a domestic washing machine with the lining, and a detachable lining can be washed separately to lighten the load.

## Making a detachable lining

Less fabric is needed for a detachable lining than for the curtain. Make up the curtain following the instructions for an unlined curtain on the opposite page. Cut the lining the same as the unlined curtain, using 1½ times the length of the track. Detachable lining tape has two "skirts," which are applied to either side of the lining. If you are making a pair of curtains, the knotted ends of the cord should be on the meeting edges of the curtains.

1 *Cut out the lining and join the widths with flat felled seams if necessary. Turn ⅜in/10mm under, then ⅝in/15mm on the long side edges. Machine stitch close to the inner folds. Cut a length of lining tape the width of the lining plus 4in/100mm. Unthread the cords at one end and knot them together.*

2 *Cut the tape ⅜in/10mm from the knotted end. Part the skirts and slip the top of the lining between them, with the corded side on the right side of the lining and with the knotted end of the tape extending ⅜in/10mm beyond the curtain. Pin the layers together.*

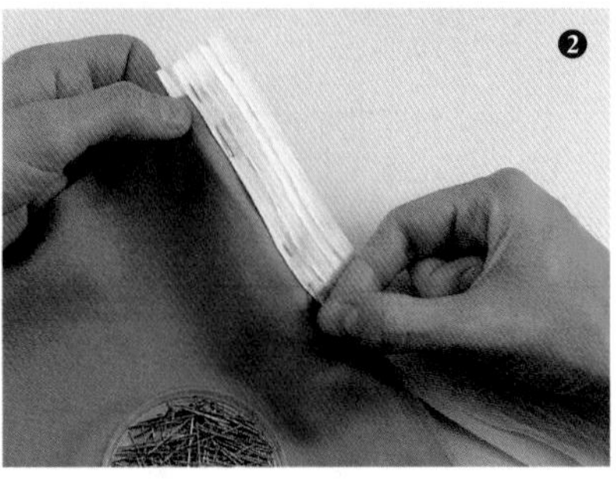


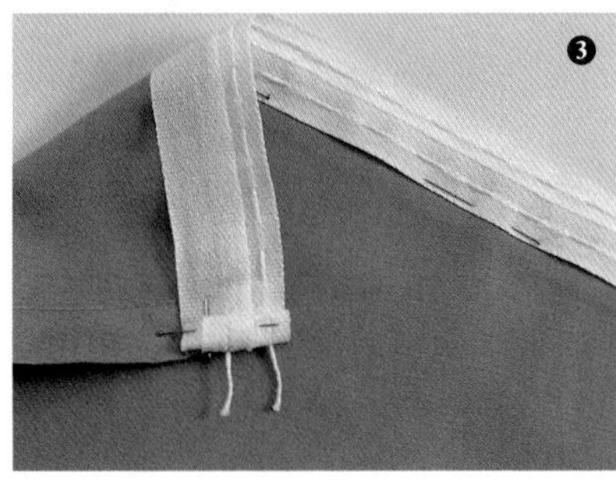


3 *Unthread the cords at the other end of the tape level with the edge of the lining. Cut the tape ⅜in/10mm beyond the lining, but leave the ends of the cord free. Turn the tape ends to the back of the lining in a double hem, and pin in place.*

4 *Stitch close to the ends and lower edge of the tape, enclosing the lining.*

5 *Pull up the cords so the lining is the same width as the curtain heading. Roll up the tape and sew to the top of the curtain. Insert the hooks 3in/75mm apart through the lining tape. With the wrong sides facing, slip the hooks through the curtain tape so that both hang from the same hooks. Machine stitch a double hem so the lining is ⅝in/15mm shorter than the curtain.*

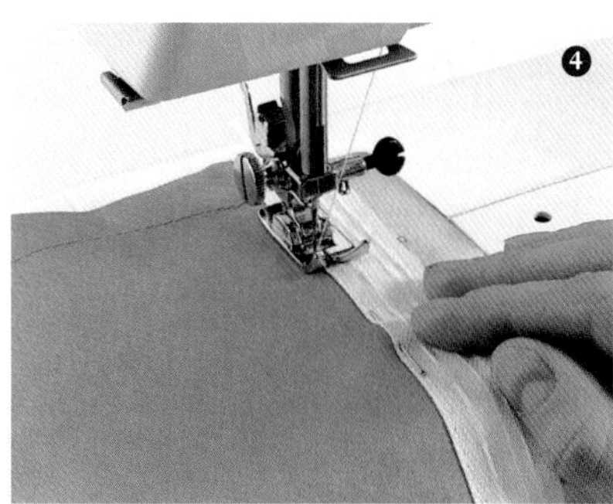

# Making unlined curtains

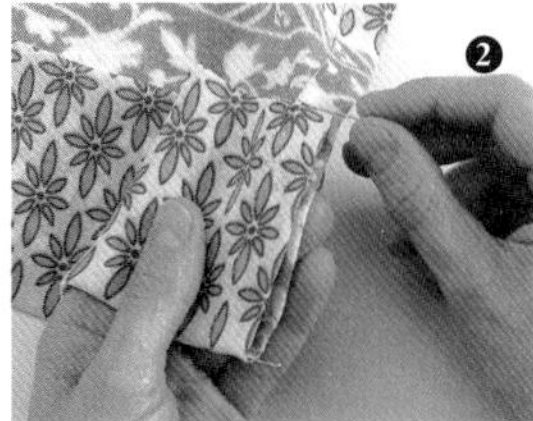

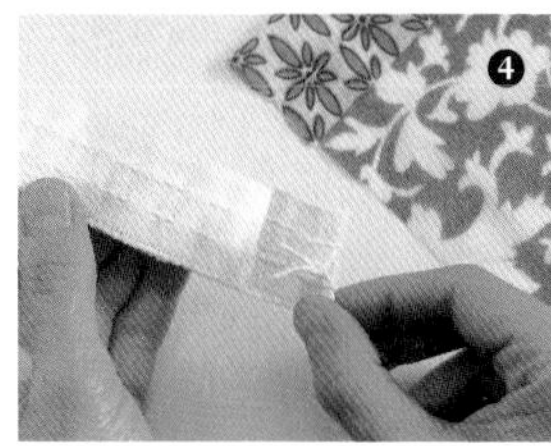

1 *Cut out the curtain and join the widths with flat felled seams if necessary. Turn ⅜in/10mm under, then ⅝in/15mm on the long side edges. Slipstitch or machine stitch in place close to the inner folds.*

2 *Press 3in/75mm twice to the underside on the lower edge to form a double hem. Mark the corner and the point where the lower hem meets the inner edge of the side hem with a pin.*

3 *Unfold the hem once at the corner. Fold the corner at an angle between the pins. Refold the hem. Slipstitch the hem and miters in place.*

4 *Press 1½in/38mm to the underside at the upper edge, or, if you want the curtain to stand above the tape, turn the fabric down that amount plus 1½in/38mm. Knot the cord ends together at one end of the tape. Turn under the knotted ends and stitch.*

5 *Pin the tape 1in/25mm below the top of the curtain, covering the turned-under edge, or, if the curtain is to stand above the tape, turn the fabric down that amount plus 1in/25mm. Stitch close to the long edges and ends of the tape, taking care not to catch in the cords. Stitch both long edges in the same direction so you do not drag the fabric in opposite directions.*

6 *Pull up the cords to gather the fabric to the required width. Knot the free ends of the cord. Adjust the gathers evenly. Slip the hooks through the slots in the tape, placing one at each end, then at 3in/75mm intervals. Roll up the excess tape and sew it to the top of the curtain or slip the cord into a cord tidy (see page 25).*

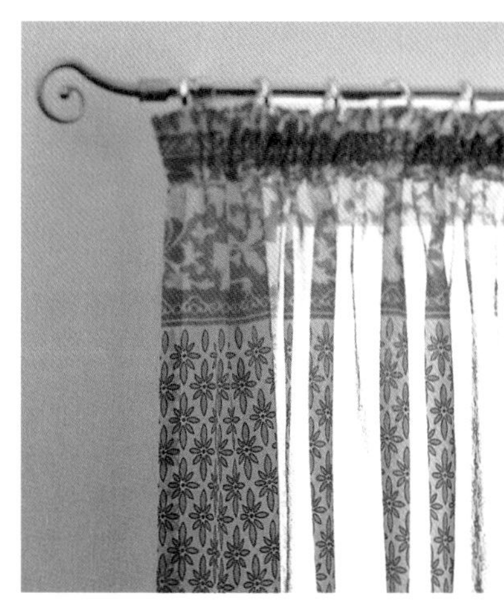

# making curtains

### *Lined curtains*

Lining curtains gives protection from dust and sunlight, and cuts down on heat loss and noise. A locked-in lining gives a very professional finish, and helps the curtain to hang well.

### *Interlined curtains*

Interlining within a curtain gives body and provides insulation. With this in mind, you could line the curtain in a warmer fabric, such as brightly-colored brushed cotton. This would be particularly effective if the main curtain was made in a figured chenille fabric or a cosy fleece. Don't use a lining fabric that is too bulky, however: you do want the curtains to fall nicely when they are hanging at the windows.

## Making lined curtains

*1 Measure and cut out the fabric (see page 32). Include 1½in/38mm top and side hems and a 4in/100mm lower hem. Cut the lining the same size, omitting the lower hem allowance. Join the curtain and lining widths with flat seams. Press 1½ in/38mm to the wrong side on the side edges. Secure in place with herringbone stitch (see page 25), finishing 6in/150mm above the lower edge.*

*2 Turn up a ¾in/20mm hem, then a 3¼ in/80mm deep hem on the lower edge. Make a mitered corner (see steps 2–3 on page 35), slipstitch the miter, and hem the lower edge with herringbone stitch. Turn up ⅝in/15mm, then 1⅜in/35mm on the lower edge of the lining. Machine stitch the lining in place.*

*3 Lay the curtain out flat, wrong side uppermost, on a large table or the floor. Place the lining on top, with wrong sides facing and the lower edge 2in/50mm above the lower edge of the curtain.*

*4 On a single-width curtain, turn back one third of the lining, aligning the fabric grains and the top edges. To join the layers together, use a double length of thread to pick up two threads of the lining fabric, then the same of the curtain fabric. Leave a gap of about 4in/100mm and repeat, catching the fabric together along its length. Keep the thread loose so it does not pull at the fabric. Fold the lining out flat again and smooth over its surface, then repeat on the opposite edge of the curtain. This is known as locking in. On curtains using more than one width of fabric, start at the seam nearest the center, locking the seams together, then work outward from the seam, joining the layers at approximately 16in/400mm intervals across the curtain. When locking seams together, stitch through the seam allowance and not the surface of the curtain or the lining.*

*5 Trim the side edges of the lining level with the curtain, then turn 1¼in/32mm under. Pin then slipstitch this in place, turn the corner at the lower edge and slipstitch for 1½in/38mm, leaving the remainder of the hem free. Check the length and press down the upper edge, and attach the heading tape.*

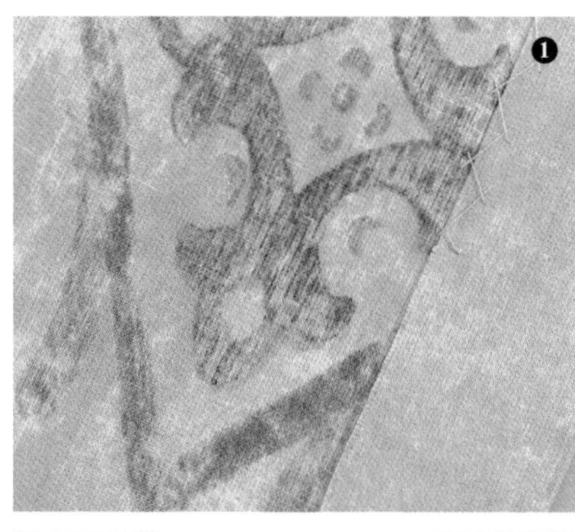

# Making interlined curtains

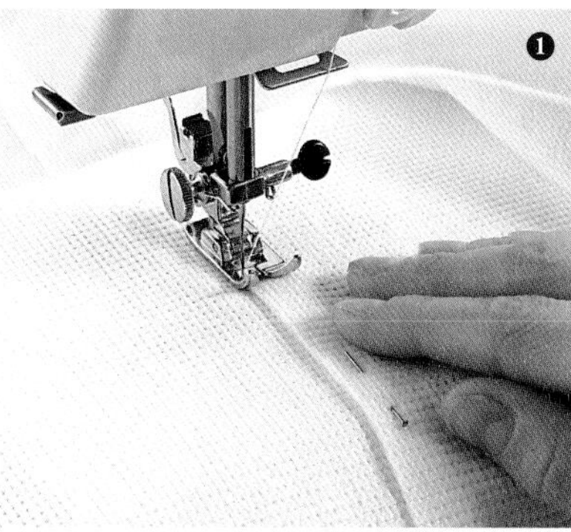

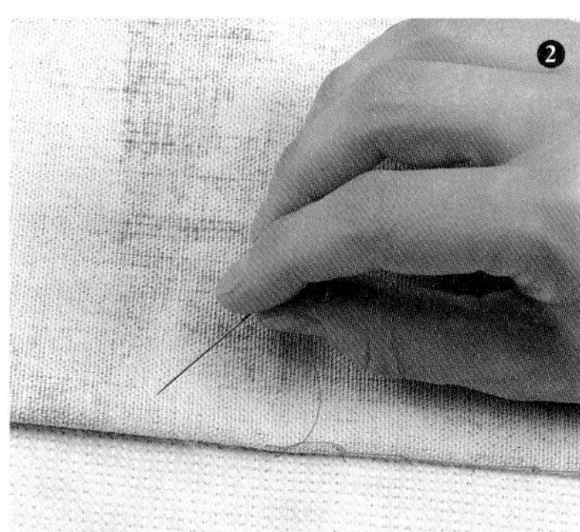

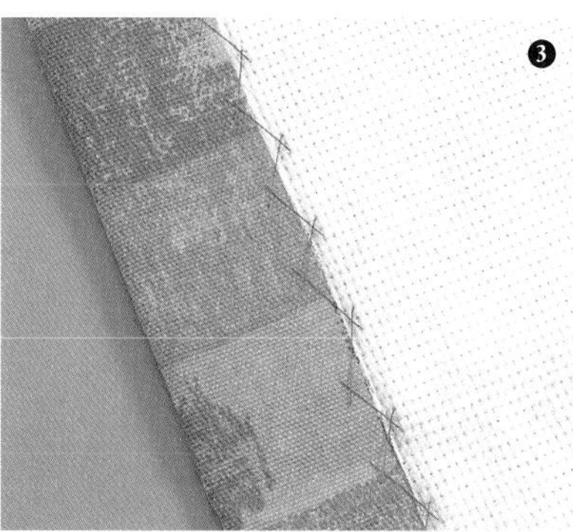

1 *To join widths of interlining, overlap the edges by ½ in/12mm and stitch through the layers with a zigzag stitch. If you do not have this facility on your sewing machine, butt the edges together and join them with a herringbone stitch. Take care not to stretch the interlining when joining it. Cut the interlining the same size as the curtain.*

2 *Join the interlining, curtain, and lining widths, using flat seams for the curtain and lining. Lay the interlining out flat on a large table or the floor. Lay the curtain smoothly on top, right side uppermost. Fold back the curtain, and join the layers together with a locking stitch in the same way as locking in the lining. Work two rows of locking on each width of fabric and along the seams.*

3 *Gently turn the curtain over so the interlining is facing upwards. Turn a 1½ in/38mm hem under along the side edges, and herringbone stitch in place. Turn up a 4in/100mm single hem, miter the corners and herringbone stitch in place.*

4 *Lay the lining right side uppermost on top, matching the lower edges. Lock the lining to the interlining. Trim the side edges level with the curtain. Turn 1¼ in/32mm under on the side and lower edge, and slipstitch to the curtain. Check the length, turn down the upper edge, and attach the heading to the curtain.*

# making curtains

### *Case-headed curtains*

Lightweight curtains look very good with cased headings threaded onto rods or sprung wire. Cut out the curtain (see page 32). For a 1in/25mm frill to stand above the rod or wire, add double the height of the frill to the length measurements, e.g. 2in/50mm. For the width, allow 1½–3 times the width of the pole, depending on how much fullness you require.

### *Double layer curtain*

A pretty valance can easily be incorporated into a simple case-headed curtain. To the length of the curtain, you must add an allowance for the hem, the circumference of the rod plus ¼in/6mm, and the depth of the valance plus ⅝in/15mm.

### *Flat-headed curtains*

Flat-headed curtains are an economical use of fabric as they are generally no more than 1½ times the width of the window. They can be fixed in place with ties, tabs, rings or eyelets.

## Making case-headed curtains

*1 Join the fabric widths, using a French seam on sheer fabrics. Hem the sides and lower edge with double hems, either with a machine stitch or slipstitch.*

*2 Press ⅜in/10mm under at the upper edge. Next, press 1in/25mm under plus half the rod circumference, plus ¼in/6mm for ease. Stitch ¼in/6mm above the lower pressed edge, then 1in/25mm below the upper pressed edge to form a channel to thread the rod through. Insert the rod through the channel, and adjust the gathers.*

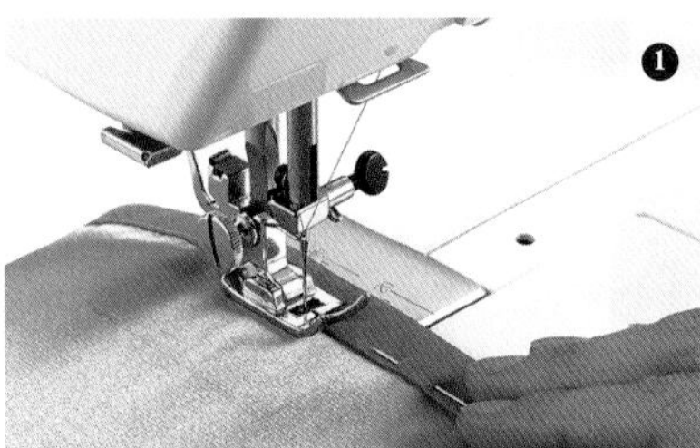

## Making scalloped café curtains

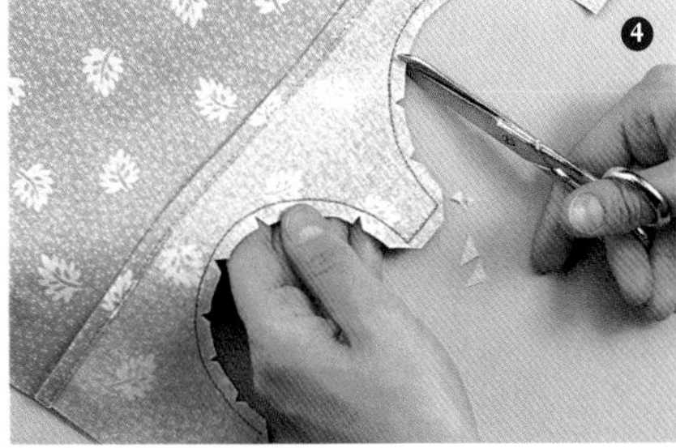

Fix the rod in position. Measure the drop of the curtain from the bottom of the rod to sill length. Add a 4in/100mm hem and a ⅝in/15mm seam allowance. Measure the width of the rod. You will need 1½ times the width plus ⅝in/15mm for each side hem.

*1 Cut out a 3⅜in/85mm wide strip of paper, which is half the curtain width less ⅝in/15mm. Label one end as the center fold. Use a pair of tool compasses to describe a 4in/100mm diameter semicircle on paper and cut it out as a template for the scallops. Fold the scallop in half and draw around it on the center fold end of the strip, matching the corners.*

*2 Open out the scallop. Move the scallop ¾in/20mm along the template strip and lightly mark its position. Continue along the template to about ¾in/20mm from the other end. If the end scallop does not fit well, adjust the size of the gaps between the scallops. Cut out the template.*

*3 Cut out the curtain and a 4in/100mm wide strip of fabric for the facing that is the width of the curtain. Join the curtain widths with a flat felled seam if necessary. Stitch a ¼in/6mm deep hem on the long lower edge of the facing. Pin the facing to the upper edge of the curtain, right sides facing, and matching the raw edges.*

*4 Pin the template on one half of the facing ⅝in/15mm from the upper and side raw edges. Draw around the template you have made with tailor's chalk. Flip the template to continue on the other half. Stitch along the drawn lines. Trim the scallops, leaving a ¼in/6mm seam allowance. Snip the curves and clip the corners. Turn right side out and press.*

*5 Press under ¼in/6mm, then ⅜in/10mm on the side edges. Slipstitch in place. Turn a double hem and stitch in place.*

## Making double layer curtains

*Make a double hem on the lower edge. Make a ⅝in/15mm double hem on the upper edge on the right side of the fabric. Fold the upper edge to the right side for the depth of the valance, plus half the rod circumference measurement plus ¼in/6mm. On one edge, mark a point with a pin half the rod circumference measurement plus ¼in/6mm below the pressed edge.*

*Stitch across the curtain at this point to form the channel. Insert the rod.*

# french pleat curtain

French pleat curtains look very stylish and suit most styles of room. You can draw attention to the attractive rounded shape of the pleats by adding trimmings. You could, for example, sew a bright button under each pleat (as shown in the picture on the right), or add another trimming, such as beads or pompoms.

A hand-pleated heading always looks very sophisticated. Rounded French pleats are also known as goblet pleats because of their curvaceous shape. It is worth investing in good-quality fabric that will hold the goblet shapes well. Here, self-cover buttons have red fabric applied and attached to each pleat, to echo the dramatic shade of the ruby red tulips on the fabric design. When buying fabric, allow twice the width plus 1½in/38mm for each side hem. Add 12in/305mm to the length for the heading and hem. Make, line, and hem the curtain as described in the previous pages in this section.

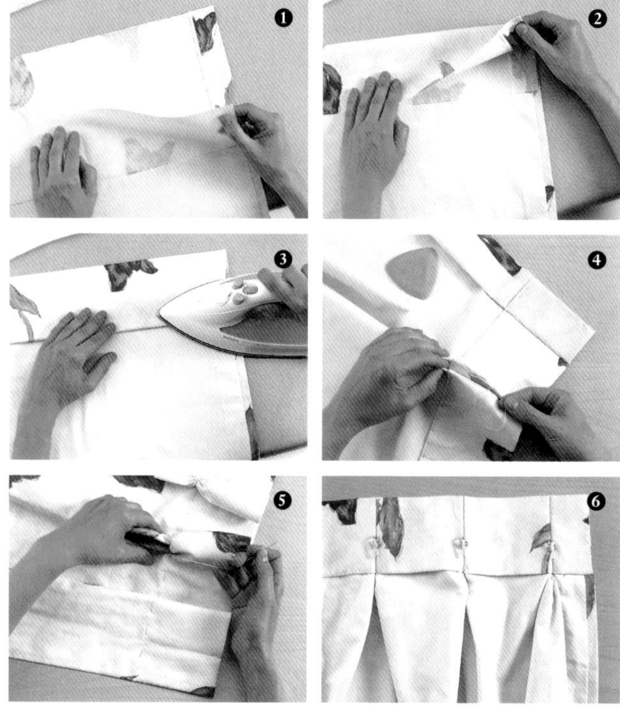

## Making a French pleat curtain

1 *Press 8in/200mm to the underside on the upper edge. Open out flat again, and cut the lining level with the fold line. Cut 4in/100mm wide strips of mediumweight, press-on interfacing to fit across the top of the curtain. Place the strips on the curtain, with the lower edge of the strips level with the fold line. If the interfacing strips need to be joined, overlap them by ⅜in/10mm.*

2 *Press the strips to fuse them to the curtain. Fold the upper edge of the curtain over the strip.*

3 *Fold the upper edge again to make a double hem. Press in position and baste across the lower edge. Slipstitch the ends closed.*

4 *Measure the width of the curtain and take 4in/100mm off the measurement. Divide the remainder into an uneven amount of sections of 4–5in/100–125mm. Starting and finishing 2in/50mm from the ends, mark the divisions with tailor's chalk on the heading on the wrong side. Bring the chalked lines together in pairs to form rounded goblets on the right side. On the wrong side, slipstitch the edges together, using a double length of thread.*

5 *On the right side, make a single stitch around the pleat on the basted line, and pull up the thread to gather the base of the goblet. Repeat to secure in place. Open out the goblet at the upper edge, and oversew to the top edge of the curtain to hold the goblet open.*

6 *Remove the basting. Sew a button to each goblet. Check the length of the curtain. Sew a metal, sew-on curtain hook to the back of each pleat.*

### *Tip*

Wadding or scrunched-up tissue paper can be slipped into the goblets to hold the shape if necessary.

6d
FOX'S
MINTS

# roman blind

The Roman blind is the most practical and elegant of window treatments, particularly when a clean and neat appearance is required. When raised, the blind lies in flat, horizontal pleats that are kept in shape by wooden dowels threaded through narrow channels.

## Making a Roman blind

1 *Measure the intended width and drop of the blind. Add 2¼in/60mm to the width for hems and 5¾in/150mm to the drop for the channels and hems. Cut out the blind and a 2¾in/70mm wide strip for the lower band that is the blind width plus 1¼in/32mm. Press under ⅜in/10mm, then ¾in/20mm on the side edges. Stitch close to both pressed edges.*

2 *Press under ⅝in/15mm on the upper edge. Pin the soft half of a length of sew-on, touch-and-close tape over the pressed edge. Stitch close to the edges of the tape. Fix a 1in/25mm high x ½in/12mm deep batten in position above the window. Use a staple gun to staple the corresponding length of touch-and-close tape to the front of the batten. Screw a screw eye into the underside 2in/50mm in from each end. Fix another screw eye ⅝in/15mm in from one end on the side of the window you want the cleat to be. Fix the cleat in place.*

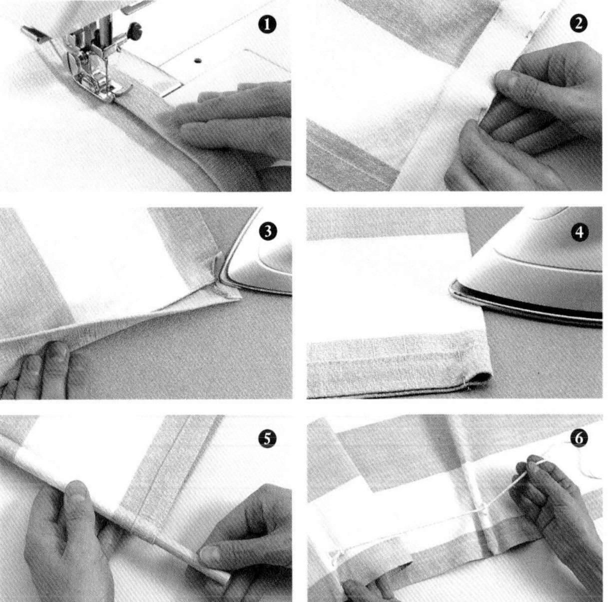


3 *Press under ⅝in/15mm on one long edge of the band. With the right side of the band facing the wrong side of the blind, and with ⅝in/15mm of the band extending at each end, stitch the band to the lower edge, taking a ⅝in/15mm seam allowance. Press under the ends. Press the band to the right side along the seam. Stitch close to both long edges.*

4 *Divide the blind drop measurement into seven equal amounts for the pleats. Working down from the upper edge, mark the following measurements on one side edge with a pin: twice the pleat measurement plus 1½in/38mm, twice the pleat measurement plus 1½in/38mm, twice the pleat measurement plus 1½in/38mm. Repeat on the opposite edge. With right sides facing, bring the pins at one set of 1½in/38mm marks together on each side edge, and press the fold.*

5 *Stitch ¾in/20mm from the fold, forming a channel for the dowel. Repeat on the other 1½in/38mm marks to form three channels. Cut four lengths of ⅜in/10mm diameter wooden dowel ⅜in/10mm shorter than the blind width. Insert the dowels into the channels and the band. Slipstitch the ends closed.*

6 *On the wrong side of the blind, sew a plastic blind ring to the channels 2in/50mm in from the side edges. Tie a length of blind cord to the lower ring on each side. Thread it up through the rings. Press the blind to the front of the batten, matching the touch-and-close tape. Thread the cords through the screw eyes above them. Thread the cord on the opposite side of the cleat through the other screw eyes. Thread the cord on the same side as the cleat through the outer screw eye. Pull the cords to raise the blind. Knot the cords together level with the cleat. If you wish, thread on an acorn and knot the cords under it, cutting off the excess.*

# swags and tails

Swags and tails can look softly draped or formally pleated, depending on the kind of look you are trying to achieve. They suit bigger windows better, because the pleating and large amounts of fabric need a certain amount of space in which to look their best. Don't choose fabrics that are too stiff, or that have a very busy pattern.

Swags and tails lend an element of sophistication to a room, and can enhance a large window that might otherwise appear rather plain. Use good-quality fabric that will hold the drapery well. Fabrics with distinct designs are not suitable, because motifs will be lost amongst the folds and may lie at what seems an odd angle, as the swag fabric is cut on the bias grain. The lining fabric will be visible on the tails, so you may wish to use a co-ordinating fabric for this.

Traditional swags and tails are constructed in three parts: the swag is fixed across the front of a shelf pelmet with a tail at each side. Try out the pattern in scrap fabric first to make sure you are happy with the effect.

***Swags and tails provide an elegant finish to this bathroom window. It is best to use plain, soft fabric to prevent patterns or motifs getting lost among the folds, or distorted by the bias cut.***

## Making swags and tails

1 *To make a pelmet shelf to support the swag and tails, saw a length of DAR (dressed all round) wood 6½in/165mm deep and ½in/12mm thick to 5¼in/130mm longer than the width of the window. Fix the shelf above the window with L-shape brackets.*

2 *Measure the intended depth of the swag down from the center of the shelf. This should not be more than a sixth of the height of the window. To make a pattern, draw a rectangle on paper that is 8in/200mm wider than the shelf width by 2½ times the swag depth. Cut out and fold the rectangle in half, having the fold parallel with the depth edges. The fold will be the center of the swag.*

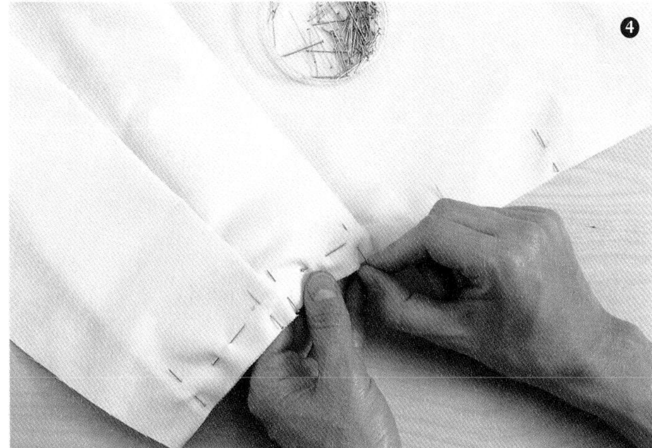

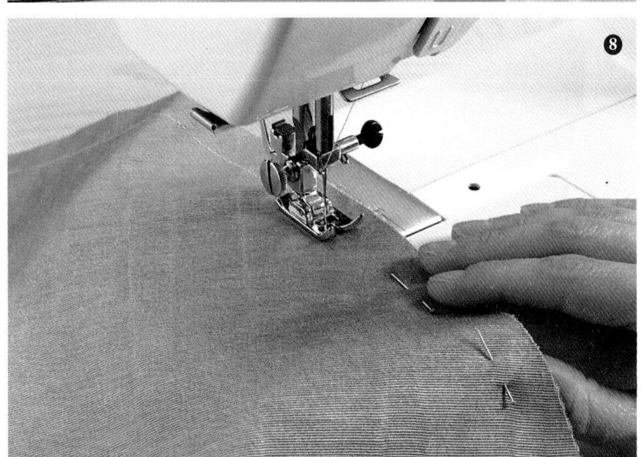

*3 Mark a point on the long edge up from the lower edge that is a quarter of the overall length. Draw a curve between the point and the lower edge of the fold line. Measure along the top edge from the fold line, and mark a point a quarter of the folded top edge measurement. Join the two points with a straight line. Draw the grain line at a 45-degree angle to the fold line.*

*4 Cut out the pattern and open it out flat to cut a swag from scrap fabric. Ideally, this should be of a similar weight and feel as the final fabric. Pin the slanted side edges into pleats 4–6in/100–150mm deep and facing upward.*

*5 To check the fit, attach the swag temporarily to the front edge of the shelf with painter's tape or thumbtacks; start by matching the centers and work outward. If necessary, re-pin the pleats or adjust the pattern.*

*6 Decide how wide you want the tails to be; they will extend over the ends of the swag. Refer back to the diagram to cut a paper pattern, and mark the grain line parallel with the long edge. Use the pattern to cut a tail from scrap paper. Mark the top edge 6½in/165mm from the long edge: this mark will match the corner of the shelf, and the long edge will be the return that goes along the side of the shelf.*

*7 Pleat the rest of the upper edge as far as the mark, with the pleats facing outward. Stick the tail around one end of the shelf with painter's tape or thumbtacks. Check the effect, and adjust if necessary. Remove the trial swag and tail, and transfer the pleat positions and any alterations to the paper pattern.*

*8 Use the pattern to cut a swag from fabric and lining, and a pair of tails from fabric and lining, adding ⅝in/15mm allowance to all edges. Stitch the swags together along the curved edge with right sides facing. Snip the curves and turn right side out.*

*9 Baste the raw edges together. Pin the pleats in position and stitch across them. Neaten the raw edges with a zigzag stitch.*

*10 Working outward from the center, attach the swag to the shelf using thumbtacks, with ⅝in/15mm of the upper edge extending onto the top of the shelf. Adjust if necessary, then hammer the tacks home.*

*11 Pin each fabric tail to a tail lining with right sides facing. Stitch together, taking a 5/8 in/15mm seam allowance and leaving the upper edge open. Clip the corners and turn right side out. Baste the upper edges together and pin the pleats. Stitch across the pleats, then neaten the upper edge with a zigzag stitch.*

*12 Temporary baste one tail to the shelf, with 5/8 in/15mm of the upper edge extending onto the top of the shelf. Fold the tail neatly round the corner. Hammer the tacks home. Repeat on the other side of the shelf.*

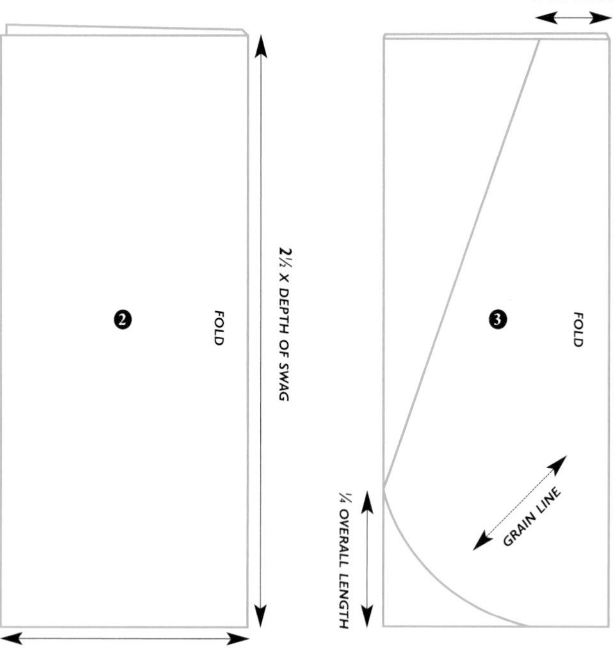

# seating

Somewhere comfortable to sit is essential in just about every room in the house, and by using the techniques and projects described on the following pages, you will be able to make the most of your sewing skills, not only to provide comfortable seating, but also to create furnishings that are unique and attractive.

Whether you choose to make sumptuous cushions and beanbags to scatter on the floor, add a little extra padding to a hard kitchen chair, or give a new lease of life to an old footstool, dining chair, or armchair, you'll be amazed at how easy it is.

# floor cushions

Floor cushions are no longer confined to student rooms. Huge, squashy cushions made of fake fur, leather, suede, or denim are very much in fashion, and add an informal air to a living room or bedroom. They are particularly good for children and teenagers, who prefer to play or relax on the floor with their friends.

Large, squashy floor cushions are the simplest form of seating to make. They always lend a relaxed and informal feel to their setting, and are ideal when additional seating is needed, at a party for example. The choice of fabric will determine their style, but it must be hardwearing. In general, floor cushions suit earthy, ethnic designs or bright, bold patterns, rather than formal, traditional fabrics. Chunky trimmings can be added, such as fringing and bobbles, or tassels or pompoms at the corners. A zipper fastening along the center of the back is most suitable for floor cushion covers, because it makes them easy to remove for laundering.

Ready-made, feather-filled 36in/915mm square inner pads are available from department stores. If you want to make a cushion that is not a standard size, it is easy to make an inner pad and fill it with your choice of filling. Make inner pads from cotton, lining fabric, or featherproof cambric.

### *Choosing fillings*

Polystyrene beads give firm support and are a popular choice for floor cushions. Fill the pad carefully, because spillages are difficult to clear up, and you will probably be finding scattered polystyrene beads for months afterward. Foam chips have a bumpy feel and deteriorate with time. Use flame-retardant foam chips only.

Feather and down is soft and resilient. Pure feather fillings are more expensive than a mixture of feather and down. Make an inner pad for a feather-and-down filling from featherproof fabric. Kapok is a traditional cushion filling made from vegetable fiber that will become lumpy over time.

## Making a floor cushion

1 Cut two 37¼in/950mm squares of fabric for the inner cushion. Stitch them together with the right sides facing, leaving a 27½in/700mm gap on one edge for filling. Clip the corners and turn right side out.

2 Pour the filling into the pad, then push it into the corners and tease out the feathers and kapok to distribute them evenly. The amount of filling needed depends upon how firm you would like the cushion to be. Slipstitch the opening closed. Alternatively, use a readymade cushion pad.

3 Cut one 37¼in/950mm square of fabric for the outer cushion front, and two rectangles 37¼ x 19¼in/950 x 490mm for the outer cushion backs. With right sides facing, baste the backs together along one long edge. Stitch for 4in/100mm at each end of the seam, taking a ⅝in/15mm seam allowance. Press the seam open.

4 With the back laying face down, place the zipper centrally along the seam, face down. Pin and baste the zipper in position.

5 Using a zipper foot on the sewing machine and with the fabric right side up, stitch the zipper in place 5/16in/8mm from the basted seam and across the ends of the zipper. Remove the basting stitches.

6 Stitch the front and back together with the right sides facing. Clip the corners and turn right side out. Push the inner pad into the cushion cover, making sure the corners are in place. Close the zipper.

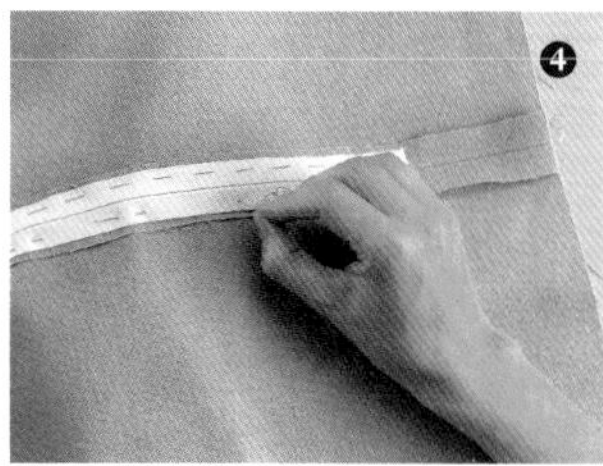

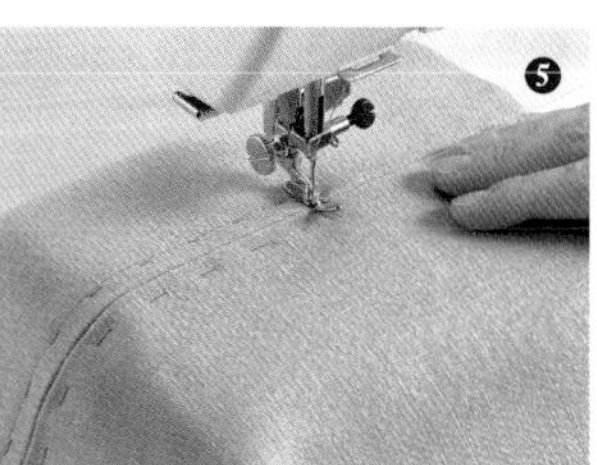

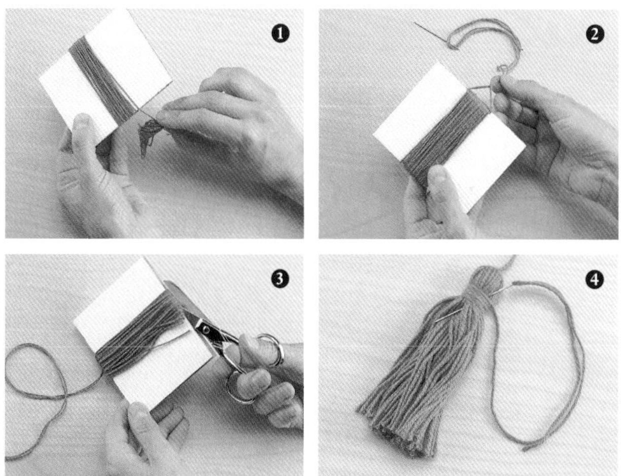

## Making tasselled corners

Add an exotic touch to a floor cushion with a tassel at each corner. Use embroidery yarn, knitting wool, or even fine cord.

1 Cut a rectangle of card 6¼ x 4in/155 x 100mm. Fold in half, parallel with the short edges. Bind the yarn around the card many times, depending upon the thickness of the tassel needed.

2 Fold a long length of yarn in half, and thread the ends through the eye of a tapestry needle. Slip the needle behind the strands close to the fold, then insert the needle through the loop of the yarn and pull tightly.

3 Slip the tips of a pair of scissors between the card layers and cut through the strands. Discard the card.

4 Thread the needle with a single length of yarn and bind it tightly around the head of the tassel, gathering the strands together. To secure, insert the needle into the bulk of the tassel to lose the end of the yarn within the tassel. Cut the tassel ends level. Sew a tassel to each corner of a cushion, using the yarn extending at the top.

# box cushions

A box cushion is tailored to cover a foam block or a deep, feather-filled, gusseted inner pad, making it very comfortable to sit on. A gusset forms the sides between the top and base. The shape of the box cushion can be emphasized with piping, or any other trimming that takes your fancy.

## Making a square or rectangular box cushion

*1 Measure the length, width, and depth of the cushion. Cut squares or rectangles of fabric for the top and base, adding a 5/8 in/15mm seam allowance to all edges. Cut a strip of fabric for the front gusset the length of the front by the cushion depth plus 5/8 in/15mm on all edges. Cut two strips for the side gussets the length of the sides by the cushion depth plus 5/8 in/15mm on all edges. Cut two strips for the back gusset the length of the back by half the cushion depth plus 5/8 in/15mm on all edges.*

*2 With right sides facing, baste the backs together along one long edge. Stitch for 1½ in/38mm at each end of the seam, taking a 5/8 in/15mm seam allowance. Press the seam open.*

*3 With the back laying face down, place the zipper centrally along the seam, face down. Pin and baste the zipper in position. Using a zipper foot on the sewing machine and with the fabric right side up, stitch the zipper in place 5/16 in/8mm from the basted seam and across the ends of the zipper. Remove the basting stitches.*

*4 With right sides facing, stitch the front and back gussets between the side gussets at the short ends, taking a 5/8 in/15mm seam allowance, starting and finishing 5/8 in/15mm in from the long edges. Press the seams open. If you wish to use piping, baste it to the long edges, joining it at the back. Snip the piping seam allowance at the corners.*

*5 With right sides facing and matching the seams to the corners, pin the base to the gusset. Stitch, taking a 5/8 in/15mm seam allowance and pivoting the seam at the corners. Open the zipper and stitch the top to the gusset in the same way. Clip the corners. Press the seams towards the gusset. Turn right side out and insert the cushion. Close the zipper.*

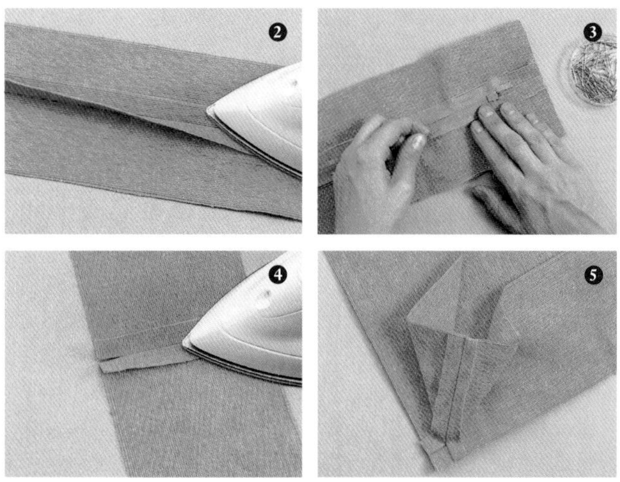

## Making a circular box cushion

1 *Measure the diameter, circumference, and depth of the cushion. Cut two circles of fabric for the top and base, adding 1¼in/32mm to the diameter. Cut a strip of fabric for the front gusset half the circumference of the cushion depth plus ⅝in/15mm on all edges. Cut two strips of fabric for the back gusset half the circumference by half the cushion depth plus ⅝in/15mm on all the edges.*

2 *Follow steps 3–4 for making a square or rectangular box cushion to insert the zipper. With right sides facing, stitch the front and back gussets together, taking a ⅝in/15mm seam allowance. Press the seams open. If you wish to insert piping, baste it to the long edges now, joining the ends at the back.*

3 *With right sides facing, stitch the base to the gusset, taking a ⅝in/15mm seam allowance. Open the zipper and stitch the top to the gusset in the same way. Snip the curves. Press the seams towards the gusset. Turn right side out and insert the cushion. Close the zipper.*

### *Tip*

To reduce the bulk in the seams, trim the allowances to different levels. This is specially important if piping has been inserted, because it will make the seam allowance layers very thick and difficult to manage. To stop cushions slipping, sew a 2½in/63mm length of sew-on, touch-and-close tape to the base of the cushion at the front and back, and a corresponding stick-on tape stuck to the seat.

## Making irregular-shape cushions

Some box cushions are shaped to fit, around chair arms for example, and must have a pattern made for them. If you intend to re-cover an existing cushion, take the old cover apart and use it as a pattern, otherwise make a new paper pattern.

If a box cushion is narrower at the back than the front, the zipper can be extended and the seams can be on the sides of the gusset instead of the back corners. This works well on wedge-shaped cushions. Alternatively, the cushion base can have a seam across its widest part with a zipper inserted.

# squab cushion

A tie-on cushion filled with a thin layer of foam adds some padding to a hard kitchen chair seat. Make a feature of the ties at the back of the cushion by binding them around the chair legs (as shown in the picture on the right). You could use contrasting, colored ribbons for this if you wanted.

## Making a squab cushion

1 *To make a pattern, cut a piece of pattern paper or brown wrapping paper larger than the seat. Place it on the seat with a weight on top. Fold the edges of the paper over the seat to define the shape. If necessary, snip the paper around the rails so it lays flat.*

2 *Remove the pattern. Add a ⅝in/15mm seam allowance on all edges. Use the pattern to cut two cushion covers from fabric. Cut the seam allowance off the pattern. Tape the pattern to ½in/12mm thick foam with painter's tape. Draw around the pattern with an air-erasable pen. Remove the pattern and cut out the foam.*

3 *Make up a length of piping for the side and front edges using the cover fabric (see pages 28–29). Pin and baste the piping to the side and front edges on the right side of one cover, starting and finishing ⅝in/15mm from the back edges. With right sides facing, stitch the covers together, taking a ⅝in/15mm seam allowance and leaving a 11in/270mm opening to turn on the back edge.*

4 *Layer the seam to reduce the bulk. Snip the curves and corners. Lay the foam cushion on top of the cover within the seam. Reach inside the cover and pin the foam to the top cover. Turn the cover right side out and slipstitch the opening closed. Remove the pins.*

5 *Cut four 1⅜in/35mm wide bias strips 18in/460mm long for the ties. Fold the ties lengthwise in half with the right sides facing. Stitch, taking a ¼in/6mm seam allowance. Use a bodkin to turn the ties right side out. Turn in the ends and slipstitch closed. Place the cushion on the seat, and pin the ties each side of the back rails. Sew securely in place, then tie around the legs.*

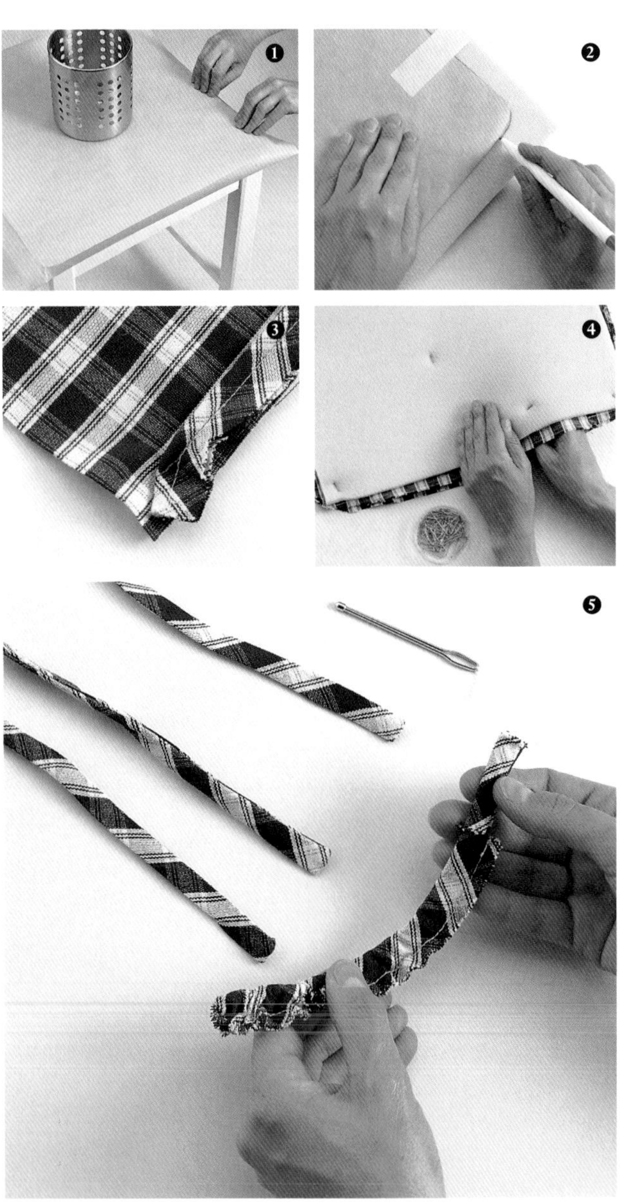

# footstools

Smart, calico-covered footstools are available from furniture suppliers ready to be covered in a fabric of your choice. Alternatively, you may wish to recover an old, tattered footstool. Remove any trimmings first. If the existing cover is not falling apart, leave it on and fit the new cover on top.

### *Slip-on footstool cover*

A slip-on cover is an instant makeover for a square or rectangular footstool. The cover is made from a single piece of fabric that can be trimmed with fringing, braid, or ribbon. Because the cover extends below the base of the footstool, this style is not suitable for footstools that have legs that jut or curve outward. A footstool of this style can be cleverly created from a low coffee table. Stick foam to the top of the table with a foam spray adhesive to make a soft, cushioned top. Place a layer of wadding over the top, fold the fulness under at the corners, and staple the wadding to the underside of the table. It is now ready to be covered.

## Making a circular slip-on footstool cover

1 *Measure the diameter and circumference of the footstool, then measure the intended drop. Cut a circle of fabric for the top, adding 1¼in/32mm to the diameter. Cut a strip of fabric for the side the length of the circumference plus 1¼in/32mm by the drop plus 1⅝in/40mm. With right sides facing, stitch the ends of the sides together, taking a ⅝in/15mm seam allowance. Press the seam open. If you wish to insert piping, then baste it to the upper long edge of the side of the cover now.*

2 *Fold the top and upper edge of the side panel into quarters and mark with pins. With right sides facing, pin the side panel to the top. Stitch, taking a ⅝in/15mm seam allowance. Snip the curves. Neaten the seam with pinking shears, or zigzag stitch. Press the seam toward the side panel. Press under ⅜in/10mm, then ⅝in/15mm on the lower edge, then slipstitch or machine stitch in place. If you wish, sew a trimming along the lower edge.*

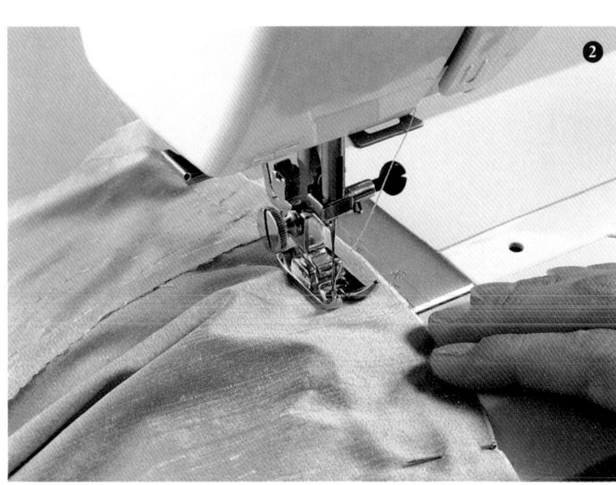

## Making a square or rectangular slip-on footstool cover

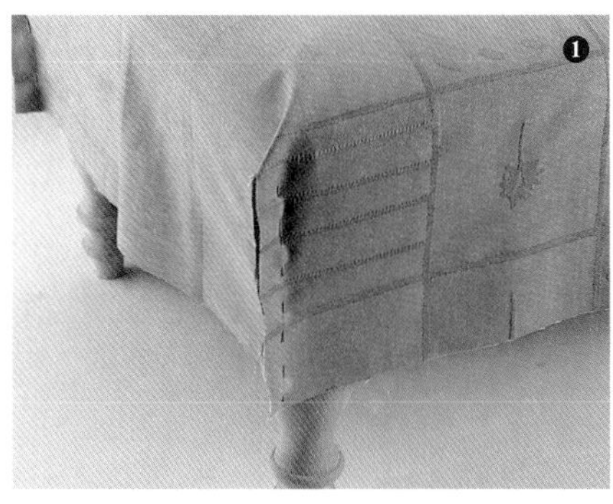

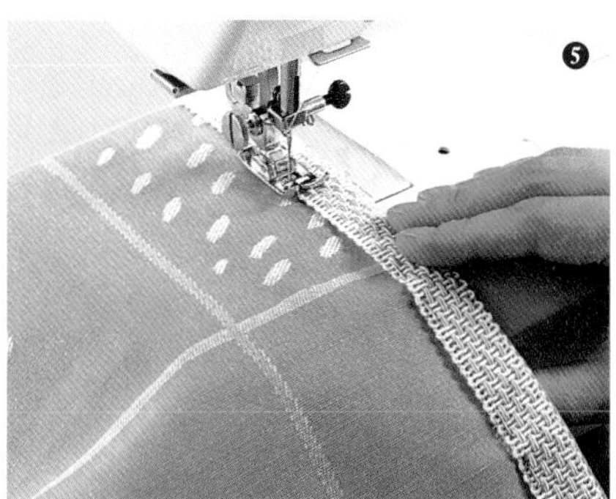

1 Measure the length and width of the top of the footstool. Measure the drop of the cover, that is how far down the legs you would like the cover to go; it should be at least 1in/25mm below the base, and can be floor-length.

2 To make a pattern, draw a square or rectangle on paper, the same size as the top of the footstool. Extend each side of the shape for the drop of the cover; these will be the sides of the cover. Add a ⅝in/15mm seam allowance to the side edges and a 1in/25mm hem to the lower edges.

3 To fit the cover, pin the side edges together with right sides facing, taking a ⅝in/15mm seam allowance. Slip the cover over the footstool and check the fit. If it is too tight, make the seams narrower. If the cover is loose, make the seams deeper. Adjust all the seams by the same amount.

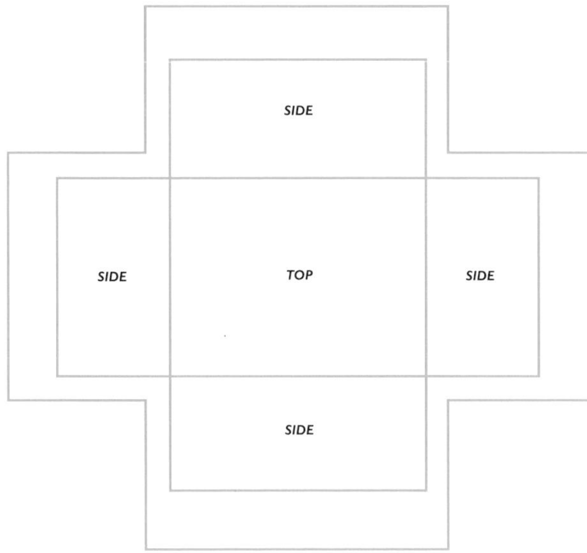


4 If the corners of the footstool are quite rounded, pin the top of the seams, following the curves. Stitch the seams as pinned. Neaten the seams with a zigzag stitch. Press the seams open.

5 Press ⅜in/10mm under, then ⅝in/15mm on the lower edges, and stitch in place. If you wish, sew a trimming along the lower edge.

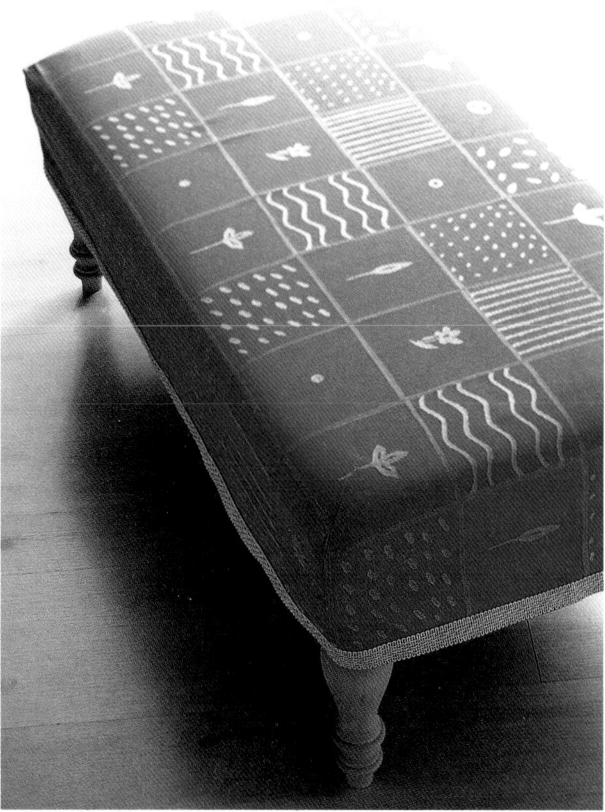

# Upholstering a footstool

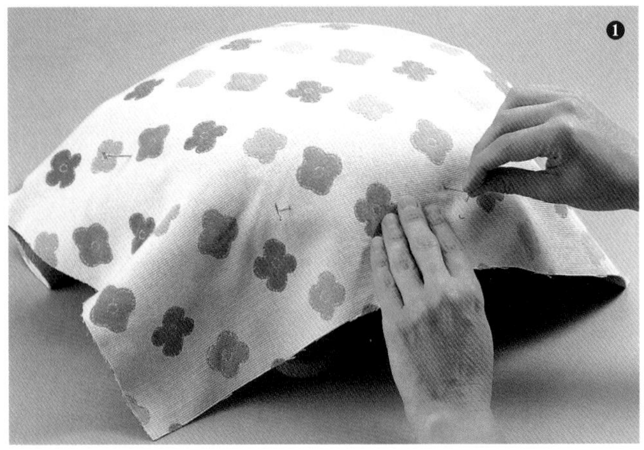

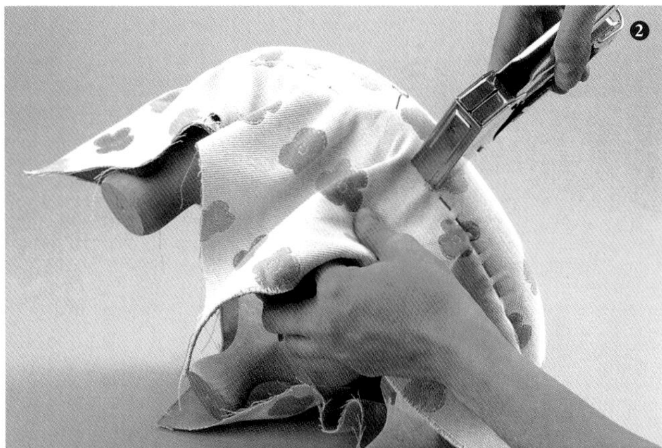

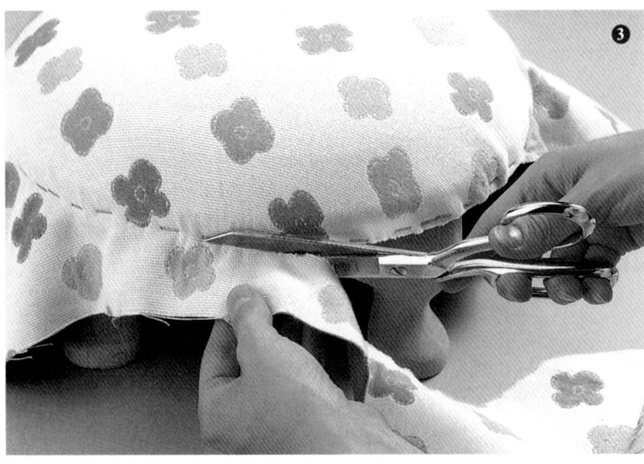

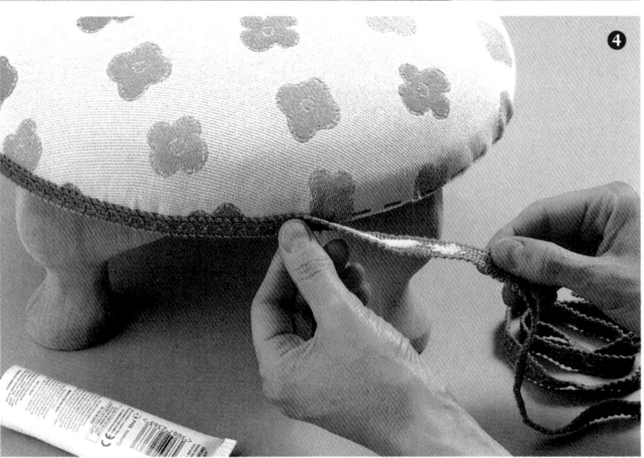

1 *Lay the fabric over the footstool, centering any design motifs, and pin the fabric in place with upholstery skewers or T-pins. Smooth the fabric outward from the center and over the sides.*

2 *Check that the fabric is lying smooth, and is not wrinkled or pulling tightly. Lay the stool on its side and staple the lower edge of the fabric onto the frame with a staple gun, or hammer in tacks close to the lower edge.*

3 *Trim away the excess fabric level with the base of the footstool.*

4 *Use fabric glue to stick braid or fringing over the lower raw edges, overlapping the ends.*

# beanbag chairs

A squashy beanbag chair is fun for all the family, and surprisingly comfortable and supportive. A fabric handle at the top makes it easy to move around. The beanbag has an inner bag to contain the polystyrene beads so that they are secure. Calico is a good choice for the inner bag, but any cotton or lining fabric will do as an alternative.

### *Animal hides and fur fabrics*

Beanbag chairs made of sumptuous leather and suede, and realistic fake animal hides are extremely expensive to buy, yet can be made for a fraction of their cost. Although there are special considerations to remember when stitching real and fake animal hides, these chairs are simple to assemble and should not be problematic.

Because animal skins vary in size, take a paper pattern with you to calculate how many to buy. Cut the skins separately, right side up, so you can avoid any surface flaws or thin areas. Weight the pattern in place and draw around it with tailor's chalk, then cut out. Stitch leather and suede with polyester thread, using a wedge-point needle for both hand and machine stitching. Press with a warm iron on the wrong side. If the iron begins to stick, cover the skin with brown paper.

Leather can be sponged gently with warm water and a little soap or detergent. Wipe with a damp cloth, then dry with a soft cloth. Brush suede with a clothes brush; some suedes are washable.

Highly realistic imitation leather and suede fabrics are available nowadays, and are very easy to work with. Make sure that the pile of imitation suede runs in the same direction on the panels when cutting out. These fabrics often have a knitted back; use a ballpoint needle to stitch with a slight zigzag stitch, to allow the seams to stretch when the chair is sat on.

Choose fur fabrics with a short pile, otherwise the chair will lose what little definition it has. Fur fabrics usually come in 60in/1525mm widths and are economical to buy. The pile of the fur should run down the length of the panels. Cut through the knitted backing of the fur and not the fur itself, cutting each piece singly to avoid distortion.

Stitch fur fabrics with a ballpoint needle. Trim away the fur in the seam allowances to reduce bulk, and pull out any fur caught in the seams with a pin. Press the fabric lightly on the wrong side with a warm iron.

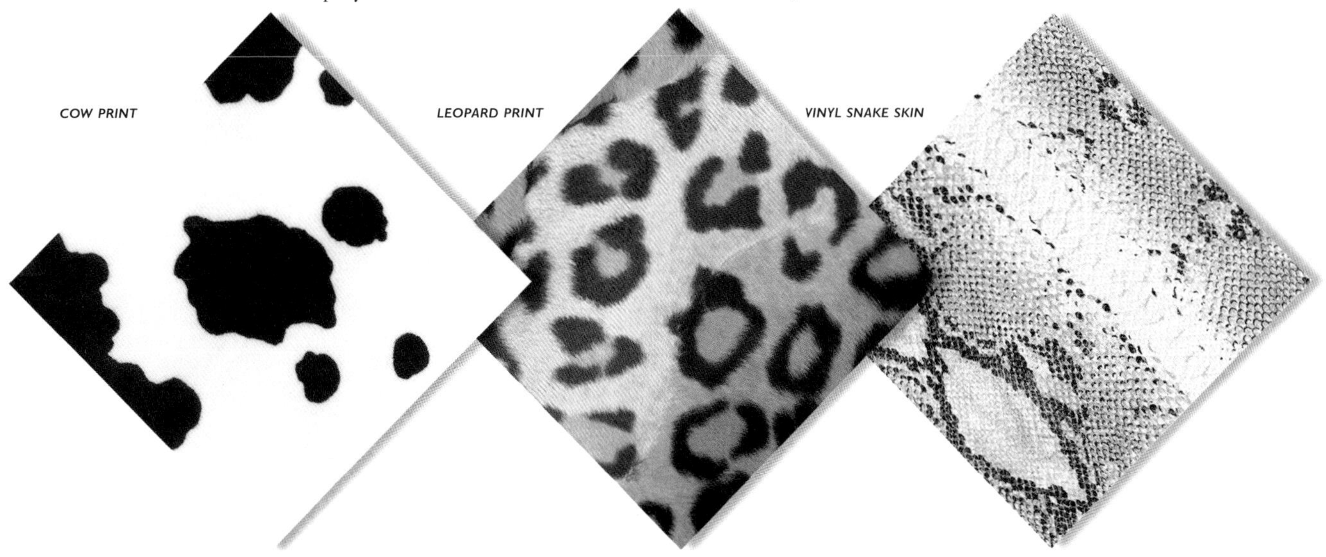
COW PRINT
LEOPARD PRINT
VINYL SNAKE SKIN

# Making a beanbag chair

1 Refer to the diagram to cut a pattern from paper for the panel, top, and base. Cut six panels, a top and a base from the outer fabric and the inner bag fabric.

2 With right sides together and taking ⅝in/15mm seam allowances, stitch the outer bag panels together, starting and finishing ⅝in/15mm from the ends of the seams. Snip the corners and press the seams open.

3 Cut a strip of fabric for the handle 9 x 4½in/225 x 105mm. Fold ⅝in/15mm under on the long edges, and fold lengthwise in half. Stitch close to the long edges. With right sides uppermost, baste the handle centrally across the top, matching the raw edges.

4 Pin the top to the upper edge of the panels, with right sides facing and matching the seams to the corners. Stitch, taking a ⅝in/15mm seam allowance and pivoting the fabric at the corners. Stitch the base to the lower edge in the same way, leaving a gap in one panel to turn through. Snip the corners.

5 Make the inner bag in the same way, omitting the handle. Turn both bags right side out. Slip the inner bag inside the outer bag. Fill the inner bag with 5cu ft/0.14cu m of polystyrene beads. The best way to do this is to form a funnel from thin card, overlapping the edges and taping them together. Push the narrow end of the funnel into the inner bag and carefully pour in the beads. Slipstitch the openings on both bags securely closed.

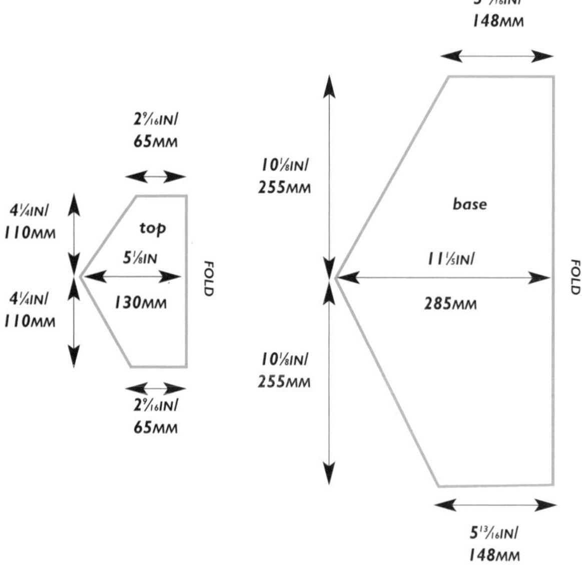


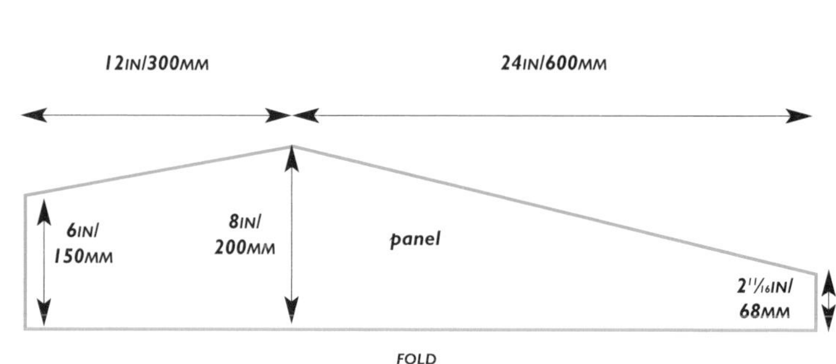

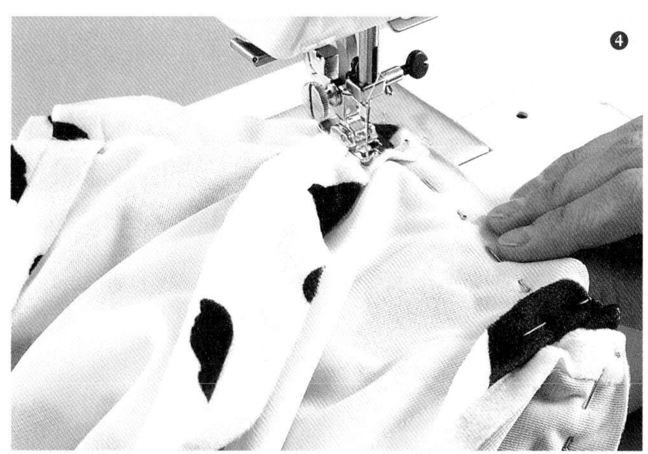
4

5

# armchair cover

Bring new life to an old and tattered armchair with a loose cover. A removable cover is not only an economical alternative to having furniture reupholstered—which can be an enormously expensive undertaking—but it is practical too, as it can be removed as often as you like for laundering.

Make sure that the chair is in reasonably good condition before you start. Piping will define the shape and give a professional finish, and a discreet zipper fastening at one side of the back will enable the cover to be removed easily. The cover fits snugly under the chair with a drawstring. Loose covers for sofas are made in exactly the same way as for a chair, but the fabric for the inner back will need to be joined. A center seam is unsightly, so have a seam toward the side edges on each side of the inner back and the outer back of the sofa. The zipper opening can be in one of these seams on the outer back.

***Reupholstery of furniture such as armchairs or sofas can be an expensive undertaking. A practical solution is to make removable covers.***

## Making the pattern

Time and care spent preparing the pattern will reward you with a perfect fit. The cover should fit smoothly but not be tight. The pattern must be made from fabric, because paper will not follow the chair's contours. An old sheet will do. If you do not have any old fabric to hand, buy a cheap remnant, such as calico, to use. Of course, if the chair already has a loose cover, simply take it apart and press flat to use as a pattern.

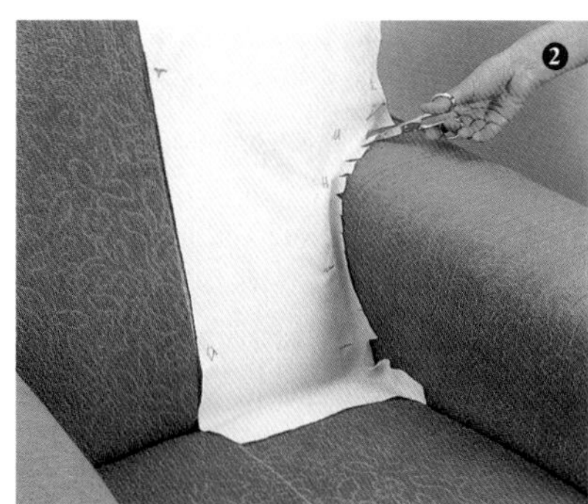


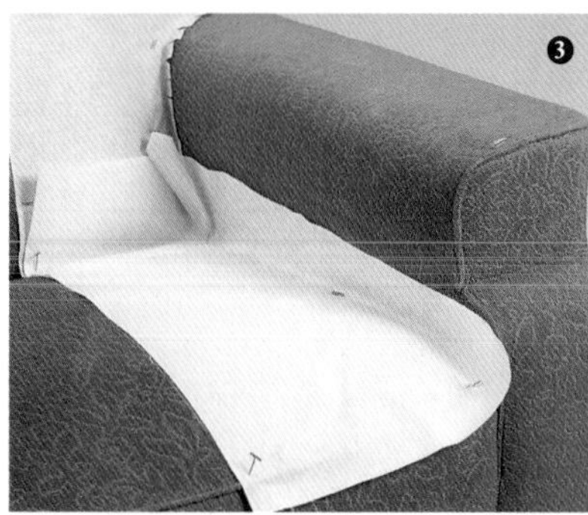

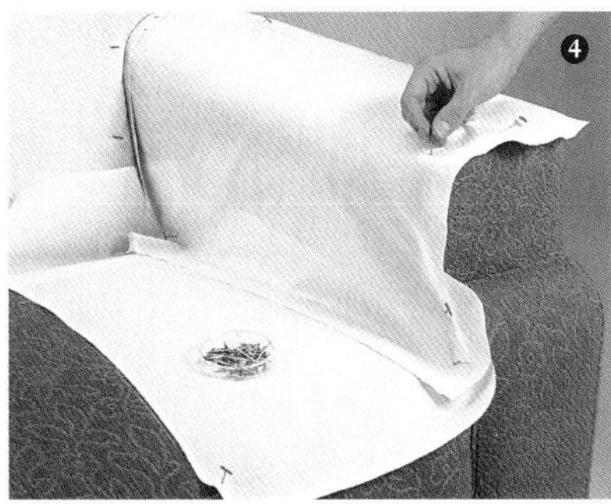

Look at the position of seams and grain lines on the chair—you will match them when making the pattern. So that the pattern-making fabric is not too bulky to handle, roughly cut it into pieces about 8in/200mm longer and wider than the area you are working on. Use T-pins to pin the fabric to the chair, because they are easier to see on the wide expanse of a piece of furniture than dressmaking pins.

1 *Remove any loose cushions. Mark the exact center of the chair on the front and back with chalk; measure this accurately, because the pattern will only be made for one half of the chair.*

2 *Follow the grain line to cut a straight edge along the length of the fabric for the inner back. Pin the straight edge to the chalk line. Smooth the fabric outward from the pinned edge. If necessary, fold any fulness at the upper corner in neat pleats. Cut the fabric to shape so it lies flat. Allow the fabric to extend 4in/100mm over the seat for a tuck-in, and leave a 1in/25mm seam allowance on all other edges. Snip the seam allowance around the arm to help the fabric lay smoothly.*

3 *Pin the fabric to the seat, matching a straight edge to the chalk line. Extend the fabric up the back and arm, and mark a 4in/100mm allowance at the back edge and taper it along the arm to 1in/25mm at the front. Trim to fit, allowing a 1in/25mm seam allowance on the front edge.*

4 *Pin the inner arm over one arm of the chair. Extend the fabric onto the seat. As before, mark a 4in/100mm allowance at the back edge and taper along the seat to 1in/25mm at the front. Trim to fit, snipping the curves and allowing a 1in/25mm seam allowance on the other edges.*

5 *Now pin the fabric to the outer arm, allowing 4in/100mm on the lower edge and 1in/25mm on the other edges.*

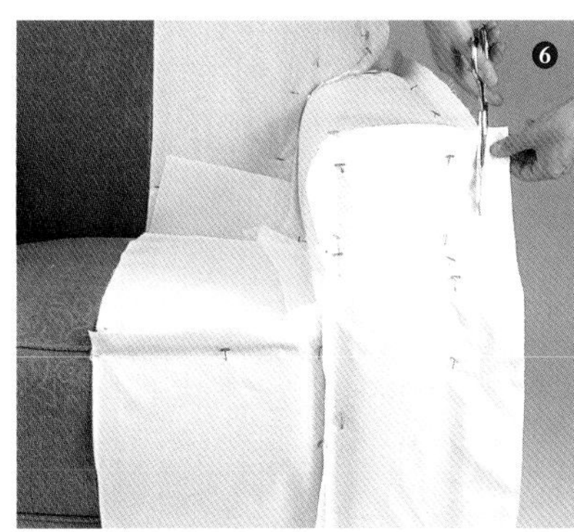


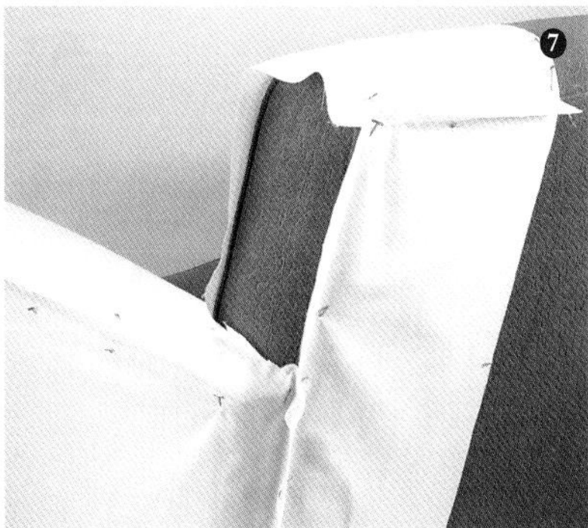


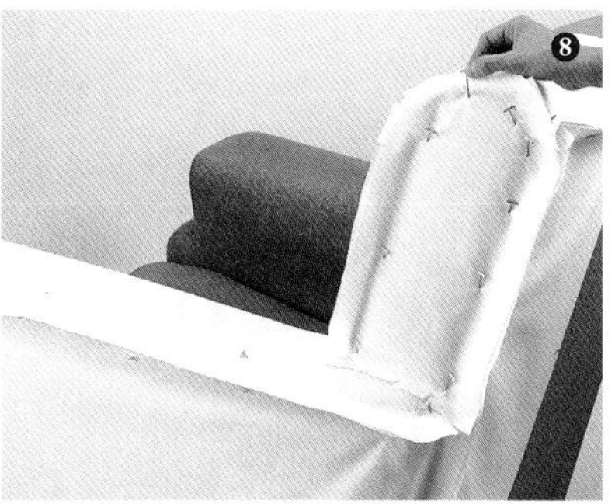


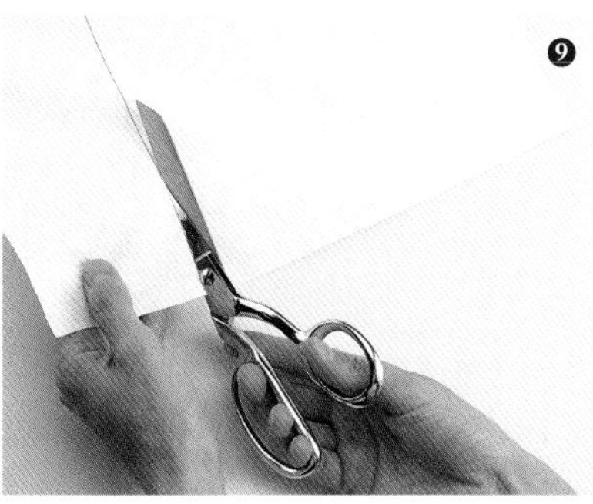


6 *Pin the fabric to an arm gusset and front gusset, matching to the chalk line. Trim, allowing 4in/100mm on the lower edges and 1in/25mm on the other edges.*

7 *Pin a straight edge to the chalk line on the back of the chair. Smooth the fabric outward and trim it so it lies flat, allowing 4in/100mm at the lower edge and a 1in/25mm seam allowance on other edges.*

8 *Pin fabric to the back gusset and trim to fit, adding a 1in/25mm seam allowance on all edges. Snip the curves at the lower edge.*

9 *Make patterns for shaped cushions. Label the pieces and mark the grain line, any pleats, and balance marks. Label the straight center edges as fold lines. Remove the pieces. Draw a line on the outer back pattern 9½in/240mm from the center back. Cut along this line (for the zipper). Add a 1in/25mm seam allowance when cutting out.*

Calculate the fabric needed by laying out the pattern pieces.

## Making the loose cover

Cut out the fabric pieces and label them on the wrong side with chalk. Pin the seams together on the chair. Clip the seam allowance at the curves. Unpin each section as you are about to stitch it, then try it on the chair again. Most chairs are not completely symmetrical, so it is important to keep trying the cover on and making adjustments to ensure a good fit. After stitching each seam, trim it to ¾in/20mm and neaten with a zigzag stitch or pinking shears.

1 *Baste and press any pleats. Baste piping along seam lines on the right side. This chair has piping applied to the back gussets and arm gussets. If basting by sewing machine, use a zipper or piping foot.*

2 *Stitch the upper end of the zipper seams on the outer back for 8in/200mm, taking a 1in/25mm seam allowance. Press the seams open. Stitch the inner back to the outer back along the upper edges. Press the seam toward the inner back.*

3 *Stitch the back gussets to the inner and outer back, starting 1in/25mm above the lower edge of the back gussets. Press the seams towards the gussets.*

4 *Stitch each inner arm to an outer arm. Clip the curves and press the seams open. Pin and baste, then stitch the arm gusset to the front of the arms, starting 1in/25mm above the lower edge of the back gussets. Press the seams toward the gussets.*

5 *Pin, then stitch each inner arm to the inner back and back gusset, starting at the outer back seam line and finishing 4in/100mm above the lower edge of the inner back. Snip the curves and press the seam open. Stitch the outer arms to the outer back.*

6 *Stitch the apron to the seat along the front edge.*

7 *Pin the inner back to the back edge of the seat, matching the centers. Stitch the back edge, starting and finishing 1in/25mm from the side edges of the inner back.*

8 *Pin the side edges of the apron to the arm gussets. Continue pinning the side edges of the seat to the lower edge of the inner arms. Stitch in place, starting 1in/25mm from the back edges of the inner arms and continuing the seams to the lower edge of the apron. Press the arm gusset and apron seams open.*

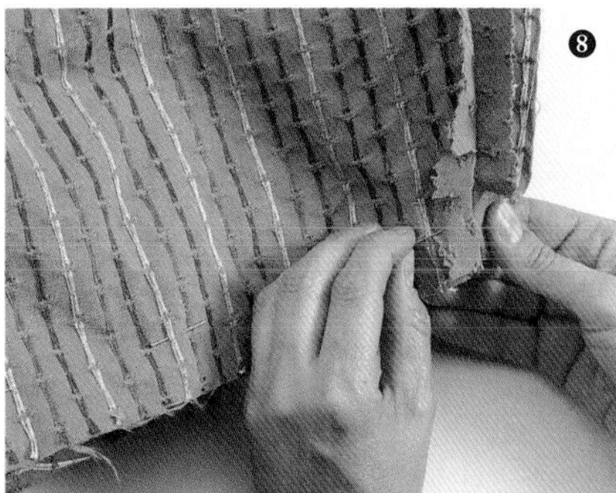

*9 Lay the lower, unstitched edges of the inner back and inner arms flat on the seat. Pin and stitch the lower edges to the seat between the seams to form the tuck-in.*

*10 Clip the corners and trim the back corners and seam allowance to ¾ in/20mm. Turn the cover right side out and try it on the chair. Push the tuck-ins down the sides and back of the seat. Pin under the zipper opening edges so they meet edge to edge. Remove the cover and insert the zippers, having the opening ends 4¾ in/120mm above the lower edge.*

*11 Slip the cover on the chair, fastening the zippers. Snip the lower edge each side of the feet to ¾ in/20mm below the chair base. Cut away the fabric and remove the cover. Stay stitch ¾ in/20mm inside the cut corners, then snip to the inner corners.*

*12 Turn under a ⅜ in/10mm double hem on the stay stitched edges. Press under ⅜ in/10mm, then ¾ in/20mm on the lower edges. Stitch close to the inner edges to form channels.*

*13 Insert a length of cotton tape or cord through the channel. Slip the cover on the chair, pull up the cord, and tie the ends in a bow. See pages 52–53 if you need to cover box cushions for the chair.*

# drop-in seats

Many chairs have drop-in seats, which can get tattered if you use them a lot. These kinds of seats are very easy to lift out and cover yourself. You can also buy reasonably priced, secondhand chairs to re-cover from scratch, replacing the old upholstery with fabric of your own choosing.

Here is a fast, no-sew way to bring new life to a worn chair by replacing the cover on its seat. Many dining or kitchen chairs or stools have drop-in seats that rest on a recessed ledge. Traditionally, a drop-in seat had a fabric cover over a horsehair stuffing, which was supported by tightly stretched webbing on a wooden frame. Nowadays, mass-produced foam versions are supported by a wooden base. The foam block is easy to work with, but not as comfortable to sit on, or as long-lasting as a webbed and horsehair seat.

A calico lining under the outer cover protects the stuffing or foam, and means the seat cover can be changed easily for washing or replacing without disturbing the interior of the seat. If you intend to use a thick furnishing fabric to re-cover the seat, check that there is enough clearance for the covered seat to fit the chair. Omitting the calico lining may help the fabric to fit. Use ½in/12mm long upholstery tacks, or a staple gun to fix the covers.

***Replacing the calico lining and covering fabric of a drop-in seat does not involve any sewing, and gives an old chair a new lease of life.***

# Re-covering a drop-in seat

1 Lift the seat out of the chair frame. Any backing fabric on the underside will need to be removed. Lever off any tacks or staples with a tack lifter or the blade of a screwdriver. Remove the old seat cover in the same way, but do not discard it.

2 Remove any calico lining. Discard any wadding or top cover to reveal the stuffing or foam. Press the old seat cover and use it as a pattern to cut a seat cover from calico and the outer fabric. If the outer fabric is patterned, experiment by placing the fabric over the seat to judge the best position for its motifs.

3 Cut a piece of wadding 2½in/60mm larger all round to fit the top of the seat and place it in position. Place the calico cover centrally on top, and smooth it over the surface. Check that the grain of the fabric is straight. Turn the seat over, holding the layers in place. Pull the calico over the underside of the frame or wood base. Starting on the back edge, secure temporarily in place with a tack hammered in halfway, in the middle of each side.

4 Working outward from the middle of the back edge, tack or staple the calico to the seat, positioning the tacks or staples about 1½in/38mm apart and stopping 1½in/38mm each side of the corners. Stretch the calico towards the corners as you work.

5 Fix the front then the side edges in the same way, removing the temporary tack first if the calico is no longer laying taut. Check that the calico is laying taut and smooth on the seat. Pull the calico over one corner, and hammer a temporary tack halfway in.

6 Fold the excess fabric under neatly in mitered folds. Run your thumb along the folds to crease them. Open out the folds again, and cut away the excess wadding and calico underneath. Remove the temporary tack and refold the calico. Tack or staple the folds in place. Repeat on all the corners. Trim away the calico and wadding to just beyond the tacks or staples.

7 Fix the top cover in the same way as the calico, making sure that the second row of tacks do not connect with the first row.

8 To give a professional finish, draw around the seat on black fabric with chalk or a china marker pencil. Cut out, adding a ¼in/6mm allowance. Press ⅜in/10mm under on the edges, and tack or staple to the underside of the seat, again missing the position of the previous tacks and staples. Replace the seat in the chair recess.

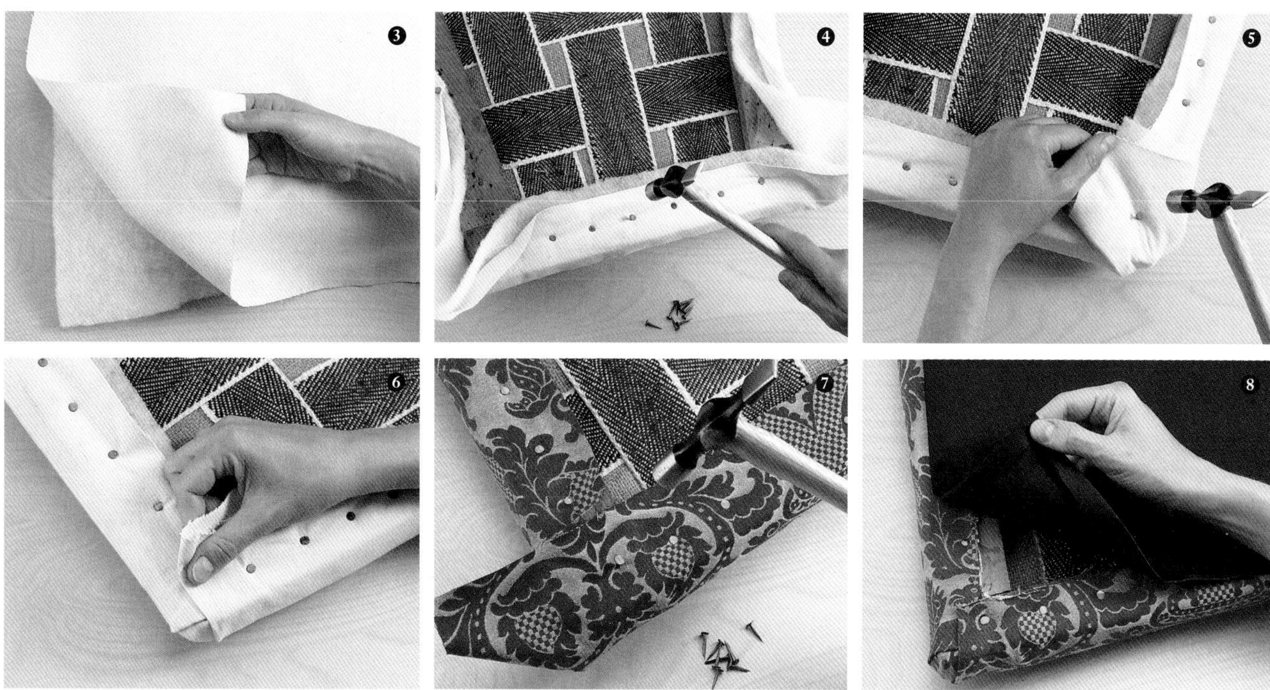

# tables

Nothing finishes off a table setting better than an attractive tablecloth, and making your own gives you scope to create something extra special. A round or oval tablecloth provides a particular challenge, but is well worth the effort, because it will emphasize the table's shape. And what could be better when entertaining than to dress up your table with a pretty set of napkins and table mats?

Of course, you can also use your sewing skills to make lovely covers for other forms of table, such as dressing tables and coffee tables, giving them a fresh new look for a fraction of the cost of new furniture.

# round tablecloths

Round and oval tablecloths are very attractive, and emphasize the curved shape of a table. The best ways to finish the edges are to bind them or have a hem faced with bias binding. (See pages 26–27 for binding the edge.) The cloth can have a turned-under hem, but avoid this if the tablecloth is of thick fabric, because it will be too bulky.

### *Joining widths*

The fabric may need to be joined to make a large tablecloth. Cut the fabric the diameter of the tablecloth plus allowances. If using two widths of fabric, cut one width lengthwise in half. Stitch the widths together with the half widths each side of the complete width, using flat felled seams, taking a ⅝in/15mm seam allowance. Trim an equal amount from each side edge of the tablecloth to make the entire width the tablecloth diameter plus allowances. Fold into quarters and cut out the circle.

### *Oval tablecloths*

To make a pattern for an oval tablecloth, place a large piece of paper on the table and weight it in the center. You may find that you need to join pieces of paper to get the size for a large table. Fold the paper over the edges of the table. Remove the paper and draw along the fold. Add the drop and any allowances to the circumference, then cut out to use as a pattern. The edges of an oval tablecloth can be finished using any of the methods used on a round cloth.

## Making a faced hem

Open out the narrow folded edge of a length of ½in/12mm wide bias binding. Cut the end of the bias binding diagonally and turn it under. With right sides facing, pin the opened-out edge to the tablecloth, matching the raw edges. Stitch them together along the crease line, cut the other end of the binding diagonally, and overlap the ends. Press the binding to the underside and slipstitch in place.

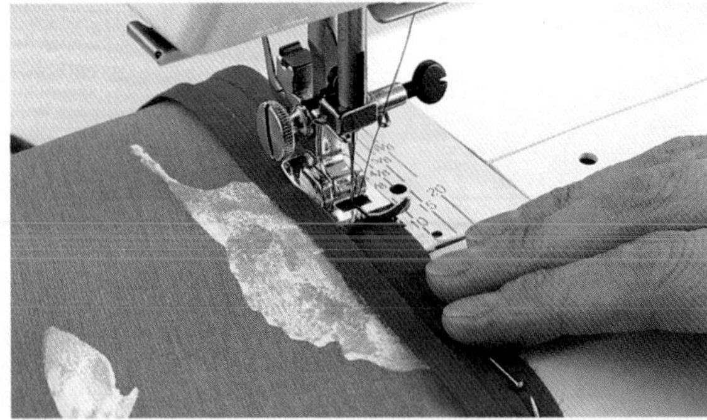

## Making a plain hem

The raw edges will need to be eased so that they lie flat. Pin up the hem. Baste close to the folded edge—machine baste rather than baste by hand (just set the machine to the longest stitch). Machine baste ¼in/6mm from the raw edge, stitching through the hem only. Gently draw up the last row of stitching so the hem lies flat. Press, then turn the raw edge under along the eased basting and machine stitch in place. Remove the first row of basting.

## Making a deep border

A deep, luxurious border on a round tablecloth really shows off the curved shape, and is a good way of combining contrasting fabrics, maybe to link different colors used in a room.

1 *Measure the diameter and drop of the tablecloth. Cut a square of paper, the sides measuring the radius and drop of the cloth. Follow step 3 of cutting out a round tablecloth to draw a pattern. Decide how deep you would like the border to be, and draw it with the string and pencil tool compass. Cut out the sections.*

2 *Re-draw the sections on paper to make patterns, adding a ⅝in/15mm seam allowance on the curved edge of the tablecloth and inner edge of the border and ends of the border. Add a ¼in/6mm seam allowance on the outer edge of the border. Cut out the pattern, fold the fabric into quarters to cut the tablecloth, and cut four borders.*

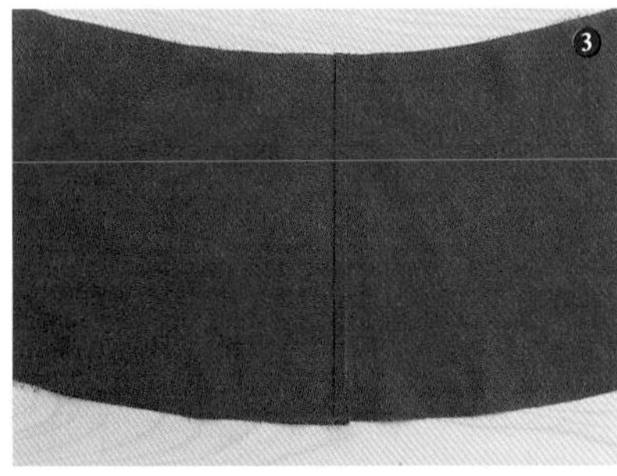

3 *Join the borders with flat felled seams and press them open. Stitch to the tablecloth, then neaten seams with a zigzag stitch. Make a faced hem on the border.*

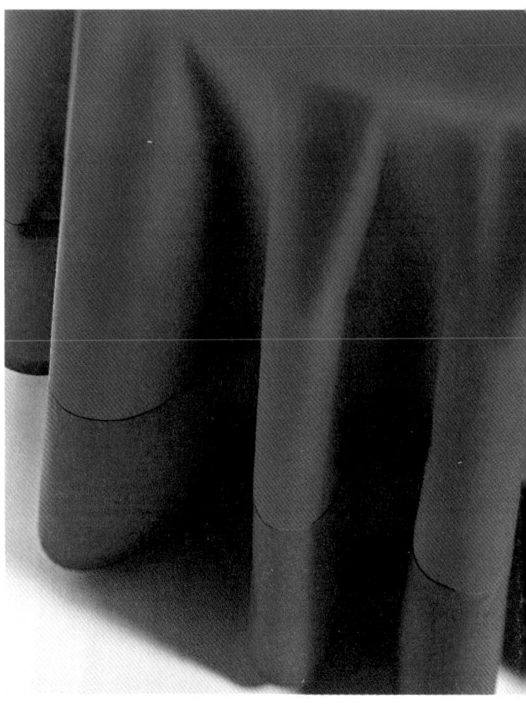

## Cutting out a round tablecloth

1 *Measure the diameter and drop of the cloth. Add twice the drop to the diameter plus 1½in/38mm for a hem. Add a ½in/12mm allowance on a faced hem. No allowance is needed on a bound edge. Cut a square of fabric to the cutting measurements and fold it into quarters. Cut a square of paper to the size of the folded fabric to make a pattern.*

2 *Tie a length of fine string to a thumbtack and fix it to one corner of the paper. Tie the other end around a pencil, holding the pencil upright on the next corner. Draw a quarter circle and cut out along the curved line.*

3 *Pin the pattern to the fabric, matching the corner of the pattern to the folded corner of the fabric. Cut out the tablecloth.*

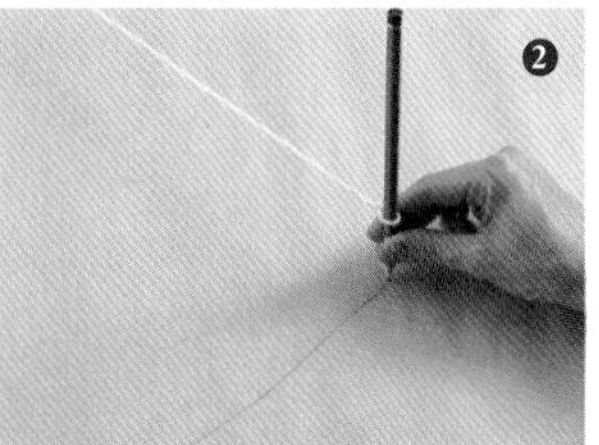

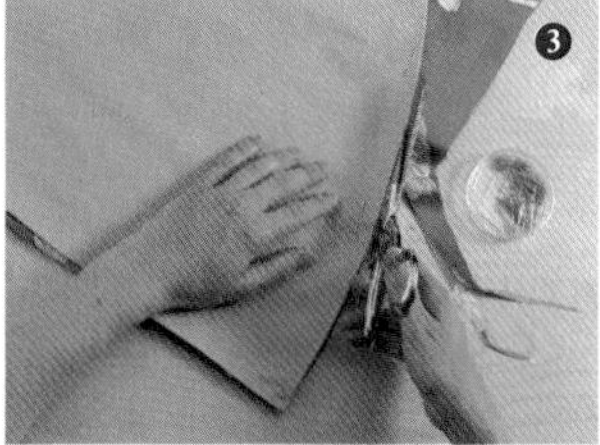

# napkins

Napkins are the easiest items of table linen to make. Their small size is ideal for decorative finishes that would be too laborious to apply to anything larger, such as a tablecloth, so you can really let off your creative steam. Make napkins from absorbent, easy-care fabrics that wash well and do not fade.

Most napkins are square and range in size from 12in/305mm for teatime napkins to 24in/610mm for dinner napkins: 16in/405mm is a size that suits both occasions. The napkin edges can be bound, hemmed, frayed, edged with lace or ribbon, or shaped with a zigzag satin stitch. Work any embroidery in one corner of the napkins before cutting out. Add ¾in/20mm hems for hemmed napkins. To round the corners and make binding the edges simpler, place an upturned glass on a corner and draw around it, cut out the curved shape, and repeat on each corner.

## Corded hem

*1 Cut out the napkin including 1¼in/32mm hems. Press a ⅝in/15mm double hem on all edges. Set the sewing machine to a wide, open zigzag stitch. Starting halfway along one side, lay two lengths of contrasting colored stranded cotton embroidery thread ½in/12mm in from the edge. Starting about 3in/75mm from the ends of the embroidery threads, zigzag in place with the embroidery threads running along the center of the pressing foot. Pivot at the corners.*

*2 Before you reach the start of the stitching, use a large-eyed needle to take the embroidery threads to the underside, then continue zigzagging, overlapping the start of the stitching. Knot the embroidery thread ends together and insert the needle into the hem to lose the ends. Cut off the excess threads.*

## Straight bound edges

*1 Cut out the napkin; no seam allowances are needed. Cut two lengths of 1in/25mm wide bias binding the same length as the sides of the napkin, and two lengths 1in/25mm longer than the sides of the napkin. Press the bindings lengthwise in half.*

*2 Slot one edge of the napkin into a shorter length of binding. Baste in place, sandwiching the napkin between the binding. Repeat on the opposite edge. Stitch close to the inner edges. Apply the longer bindings to the remaining edges in the same way, turning the ends under. Stitch close to the inner edges.*

## Scalloped edge

1 For a 16in/405mm square napkin, cut a strip of paper for a template 16 x 1½in/405 x 38mm. Draw a line lengthwise along the centre, and starting ¾in/20mm from one end, use a tool compass to describe a semicircle with a ¾in/20mm radius. Continue describing semicircles along the centre line to form a row of eight scallops. Cut out the scallops.

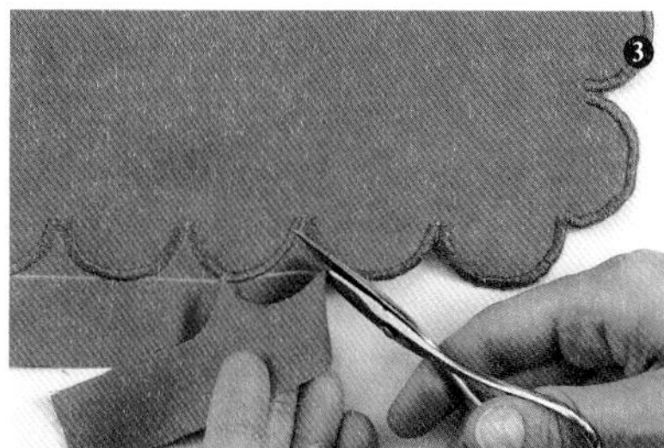


2 Cut a 18in/460mm square of fabric. Use an air-erasable pen or tailor's chalk to draw a 1in/25mm deep margin around the outer edges. Butt the scalloped edge of the template up to the drawn line on one edge, and draw around the scallops with the air-erasable pen or tailor's chalk. Repeat on the other edges.

3 Cut four 18 x 2⅜in/460 x 60mm strips of stitch-and-tear interfacing, and pin them under the edges of the napkin to reinforce the stitching. Set the sewing machine to a wide, close zigzag stitch, and thread the machine with machine embroidery thread. On the right side, work the zigzag stitch along the scalloped lines. Carefully tear away the interfacing. Use a small, sharp pair of scissors to trim away the excess fabric.

## Lace edge

*Choose a flat lace edging about 1in/25mm wide. Neaten the raw edge of the lace with a zigzag stitch. Cut out the napkin with a ⅜in/10mm hem. Stitch a ¼in/6mm deep double hem on all edges. Pin the straight edge of the lace under the hemmed edges, folding under the fullness at the corners in neat miters. Overlap the ends of the lace at a corner for neatness, and cut off the excess lace. Stitch in place.*

## Frayed edge

*Cut the napkin to size from a loosely woven fabric, cutting carefully along the grain lines. Machine zigzag stitch 1in/25mm in from the edges. Pull out the threads as far as the stitching on all edges. Remove the threads one at a time to prevent tangling.*

# table mats

Fabrics for table mats need to be durable and washable, specially if they are to be used daily. Mats made from sturdy, heavyweight fabrics will help protect the table, and a layer of curtain interlining will give added protection from heat, and also slightly cushion the crockery.

Because only small amounts of fabric are needed, making a set of table mats is a good way of using up leftover tablecloth fabric. A table mat should be large enough to take a complete place setting: 19 x 14in/480 x 355mm is a standard size. For just a dinner plate, which is usually 10in/255mm diameter, a 14 x 12in/355 x 305mm mat would be suitable, but measure your own dinner service, because the size may be different.

The easiest method of finishing a mat that has a layer of curtain interlining is to bind the edges with bias binding; there is no need to add a seam allowance. If you prefer to bag out the mat, add ⅝in/15mm seam allowances to all edges and carefully trim away the interlining in the seam allowances after stitching, to reduce the bulk. Add a 1in/25mm hem to single-layer mats.

To fuse practicality with a decorative touch, make a center panel for the table mat from a hardwearing fabric, then add a strip of pretty fabric to the side edges—check that all the fabrics have compatible washing instructions. Either hem the outer edges or bag out the mat with a lining. For a quick and pretty look, hem a rectangle of linen and sew a row of pearl buttons along one side edge; linen can be washed at high temperatures.

Cut shaped mats from PVC for children's mealtimes—a chunky automobile or chubby teddy is very popular, and the mats just need to be wiped clean after use. Alternatively, make a mat from fabric featuring a favorite cartoon character, and fix a layer of transparent plastic on top with a popper at each corner. The plastic can be wiped clean and removed when the fabric mat needs washing.

## Bias-bound quilted table mat

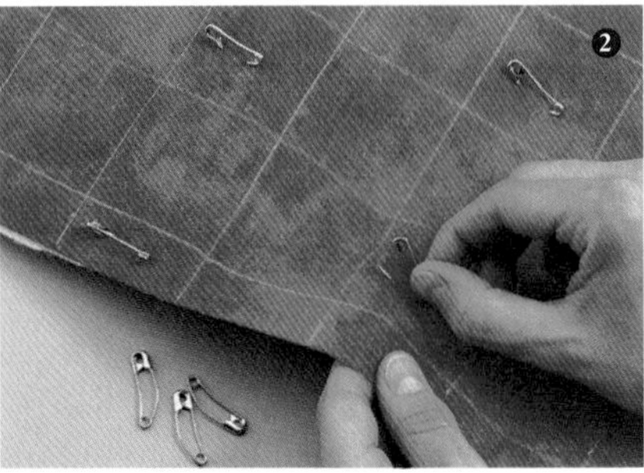

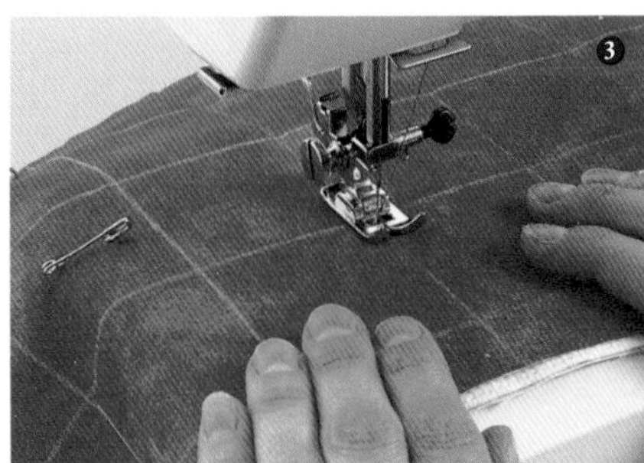

Ready-quilted fabric is available from fabric departments and can be used for table mats, but it is very easy to quilt fabric yourself, which means that you have a wider choice of fabrics to use. Rounded corners are simple to bind.

1 *To quilt the fabric yourself, cut two rectangles of fabric and one of curtain interlining for the front and back 19¾ x 14¾in/505 x 375mm. Sandwich the interlining between the fabric pieces, with the right sides facing outward.*

2 *Draw a grid of 2in/50mm squares with tailor's chalk on the top fabric. Use curved basting pins to pin the layers smoothly together.*

3 *Starting at the center, stitch along the vertical drawn lines, stitching down one line,*

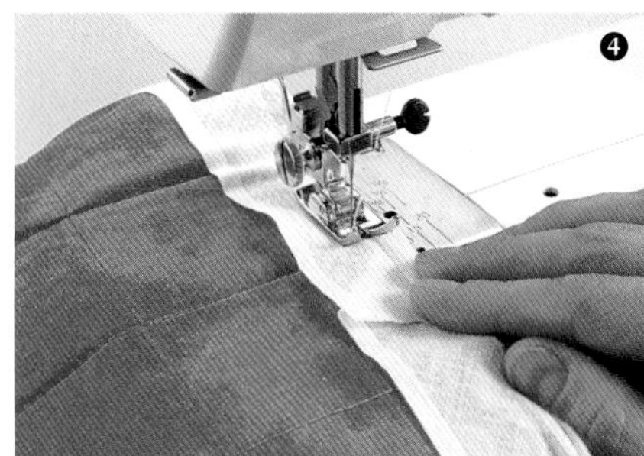


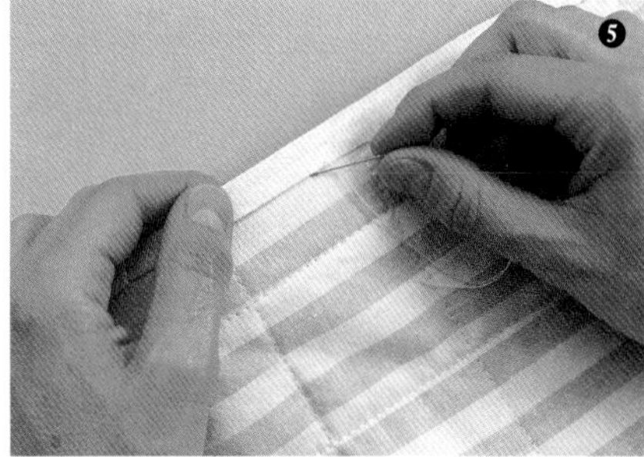


up the next and so on. Turn the mat and stitch the horizontal lines in the same way. Cut the mat to 19 x 14in/485 x 355mm. To round the corners, place a glass upside down on one corner and draw around it with an air-erasable pen. Cut out, then repeat on the other corners.

4 Open out the narrow edge of 1in/25mm wide bias binding. Turn under one end diagonally, and pin the binding to the outer mat edge with the right sides facing, taking a ¼in/6mm seam allowance. Overlap the binding ends, stitching along the foldline of the binding.

5 Clip the corners to reduce the bulk in the seam allowance. Turn the binding to the underside of the mat. Pin and slipstitch the binding in place.

# dressing table

The classic, kidney-shaped dressing table looks right in either a traditional or a retro-style bedroom, depending upon the fabric used. Original dressing tables can be made over, or bought plain and ready to be upholstered. These are usually made of chipboard. They generally have a curtain rail under the table top.

## Making a dressing table cover

Remove any original covering if you are re-covering an existing dressing table. Check the condition of the rail, and replace it if necessary. This top has a deep pleated frill over a gathered skirt, which has a front opening. Take a ⅝in/15mm seam allowance throughout.

1 *Make a pattern for the table top by turning it upside down and drawing around it on paper. Add a ⅝in/15mm seam allowance. Use the pattern to cut the top from fabric, centering any pattern design if necessary. Cut one top from lining. (Inexpensive lightweight cotton fabric would be suitable for the lining if you want to economize on the main fabric.)*

2 *Measure the circumference of the table top. Cut 10½in/270mm wide strips of fabric for the top frill; the strips will be joined end to end, and the finished length should be twice the top circumference. Add seam allowances for joining the strips. Join the strips end to end with flat felled seams to form a ring. Press under ⅜in/10mm, then ⅝in/15mm on one long edge. Stitch close to the inner pressed edge.*

3 *Pin the upper raw edge into ½in/12mm deep pleats 1in/25mm apart, all laying in the same direction. With right sides facing, pin the frill to the top. Adjust the pleats if needed. Stitch in place.*

4 *With right sides facing, pin and stitch the lining to the fabric top, sandwiching the frill: leave a 10in/250mm gap to turn through. Trim the seam allowance and snip the curves. Turn right side out and slipstitch the opening closed.*

5 *Measure the drop of the skirt from the top of the rail to the floor. Cut widths of fabric for the skirt that are the drop of the skirt plus 2in/50mm, the widths will be joined to make a continuous length that should be twice the top circumference plus a 1in/25mm hem at each end. Add ⅝in/15mm seam allowances for joining the widths. Join the widths with flat felled seams.*

6 *Press under ⅜in/10mm, then ⅝in/15mm on the ends and lower edge of the skirt. Slipstitch or machine stitch close to the inner pressed edges. (See page 35 for how to make mitered corners.)*

3

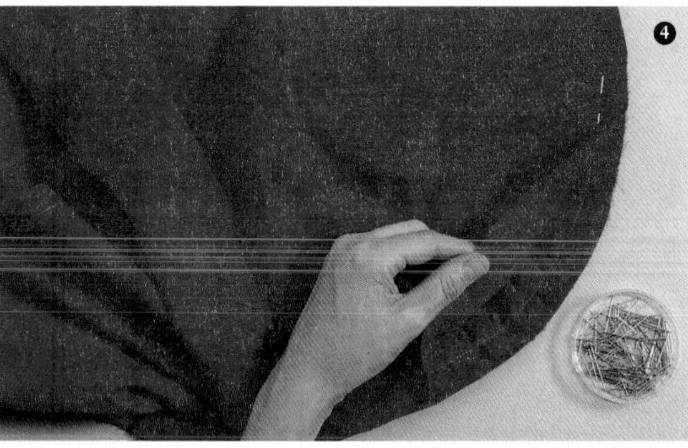
4

7 *Press the upper edge to the wrong side for 1in/25mm. Pin standard curtain tape along the upper edge, enclosing the raw edges. Turn under the ends of the tape and stitch close to the edges, taking care not to catch in the cords.*

8 *Pull up the cords to gather the fabric to fit around the table. Knot the free ends of the cords and adjust the gathers evenly. Slip curtain hooks through the slots in the tape, placing one at each end and at 3in/75mm intervals.*

9 *Hook the skirt onto the rail, positioning the opening edges at the front. Slip the fabric top onto the top of the table. Cut the seam allowance off the paper pattern for the top, and take it to a glazier to use as a template to cut a piece of glass to fit the table top. Make sure that you have the edges beveled. Place the glass carefully on top of the dressing table.*

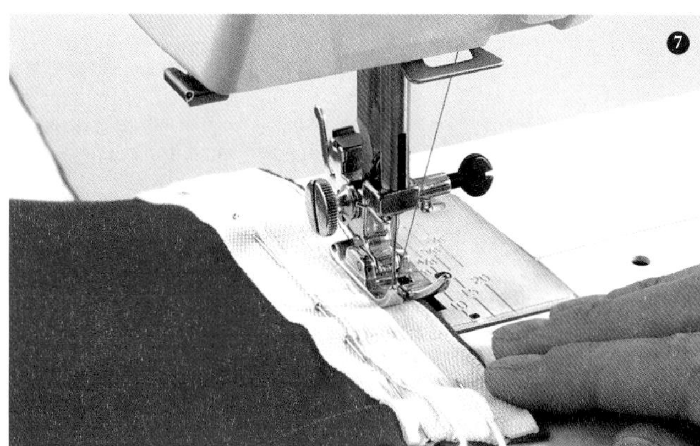


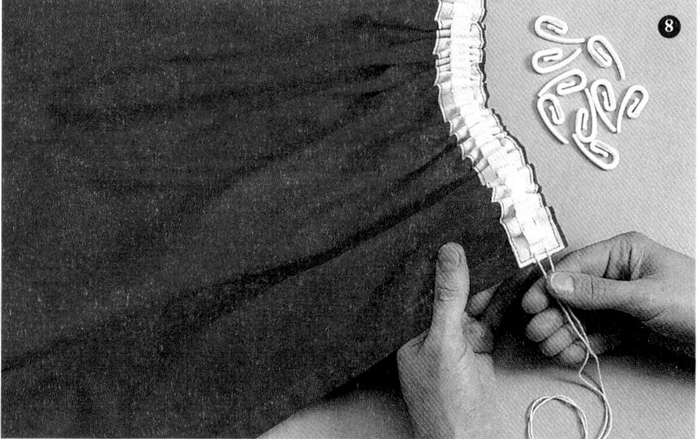

# fitted table cover

Put a shabby coffee table to new use by making a neat fitted cover—the deep pleats at the front of this table (see picture on the right) make the interior accessible for storing books and other items. The top is edged with co-ordinating piping, either your own or ready-made. Use fabrics that hold their shape.

## Making a fitted table cover

Measure the width and depth of the table top, and measure the drop of the table. Use a flat felled seam if you need to join fabric for the skirt. Take ⅝in/15mm seam allowances throughout.

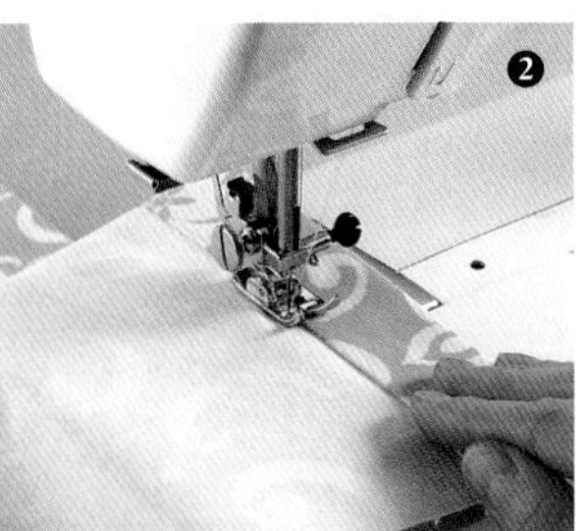

1 *Cut a square or rectangle of fabric for the top that is the table width plus 1¼in/32mm by the depth plus 1¼in/32mm. Pin and baste piping to the outer edge on the right side, snipping the seam allowance of the piping at the corners. Join the piping on the back edge (see pages 28–29).*

2 *For the back and sides skirt, cut a rectangle of fabric twice the table depth plus the width, plus 8¼in/210mm by the drop plus 2⅜in/60mm. Cut a rectangle or square for the front skirt the table width plus 8¼in/210mm by the drop plus 2⅜in/60mm. To hem, press ¾in/20mm under, then 1in/25mm on one long lower edge of the skirts. Stitch close to the inner pressed edges.*

3 *Stitch the front skirt to the back and sides skirt with French seams to form a continuous length. With the right side face up, mark both edges of the front skirt with a pin 3½in/88mm from one seam. Fold and press the front at the pin mark to lie flat on the side skirt. Baste across the upper edge, and repeat on the other end of the front skirt.*

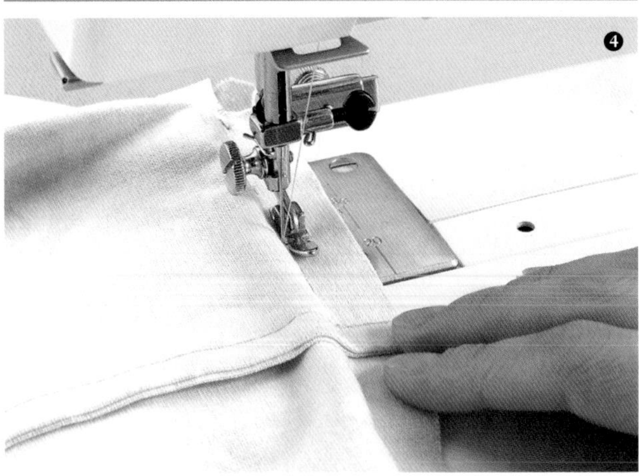

4 *With the right sides facing, pin and baste the skirt to the top, matching the pleats to the front corners. Snip the skirts at the corners. Stitch in place using a zipper foot, pivoting the stitching at the corners. Clip the corners, and neaten the seam with a zigzag stitch or pinking shears. Press the table cover, adjusting the top seam toward the skirt. Turn right side out and slip the cover over the table.*

# beds

The bedroom, and especially the bed, are where soft furnishings really come into their own, helping to create a delightfully peaceful atmosphere, and providing real comfort to encourage sleep or simply relaxation.

By using the techniques shown on the following pages, you will be able to create a wonderful selection of attractive soft furnishings for your bedroom, from pretty bordered sheets, through decorated pillowcases and cushions, to beautiful comforter covers and bedspreads. And for that final, slightly exotic touch, why not enclose the head of your bed with a rounded, curtained corona, and drift off to sleep lulled by thoughts of Arabian nights?

# paisley border sheet

Appliqué applied by the sewing machine gives a very professional finish. This sheet (see picture on the right) is edged with a colorful border of paisley shapes, which are highlighted with simple hand embroidery. The same type of border can also be applied to a ready-made sheet.

## Making a paisley border sheet

The measurements given here are for making a single sheet. To make a double sheet, cut the sheet 92 x 101½in/2350 x 2590mm and the border 91¼ x 8⅛in/2330 x 210mm.

1 *Cut a rectangle of white sheeting 98 x 67in/2490 x 1700mm. Press ⅜in/10mm, then ⅝in/15mm to the wrong side on the long side edges. Stitch close to the inner pressed edge. Press ⅜in/10mm then 2in/50mm to the wrong side on the short lower edge. Stitch close to the inner pressed edge.*

2 *Cut a strip of turquoise sheeting for the border 66¼ x 8⅛in/1680 x 210mm. Press the border lengthwise in half, with the wrong sides facing. Open the border out flat again, and press under ⅜in/10mm on one long edge.*

3 *Make a paper template of the paisley pattern and draw around it seven times on the paper backing side of bonding web. Apply the paisley motifs to two striped fabrics, and cut them out. Working outward from the center, refer to the bonding web technique on page 29 to apply the motifs in alternate directions and colorways to the unpressed half of the border 4⅛in/105mm apart and 1in/25mm in from the long raw edge.*

4 *Set the sewing machine to a close zigzag stitch ⅛in/3mm wide. Stitch along the edges of the motifs to conceal the raw edges. Pull the end threads to the back of the border, and knot them together.*

5 *Thread a crewel needle with six strands of stranded cotton embroidery thread. Embroider three stars on each paisley with six straight stitches radiating outward from the dots. Press the paisleys face down on a towel so the embroidery is not flattened.*

6 *Fold the ends of the border along the foldline with right sides facing. Stitch the ends, taking a ⅝in/15mm seam allowance. Clip the corners and turn right side out. With right sides facing, stitch the border to the upper edge of the sheet, matching the raw edges and taking a ⅝in/15mm seam allowance. Clip the corners. Press the seam towards the border.*

7 *Re-press the border in half along the center foldline. Pin the pressed edge of the back of the border along the seam, enclosing the seam allowance. On the right side, topstitch close to the seam.*

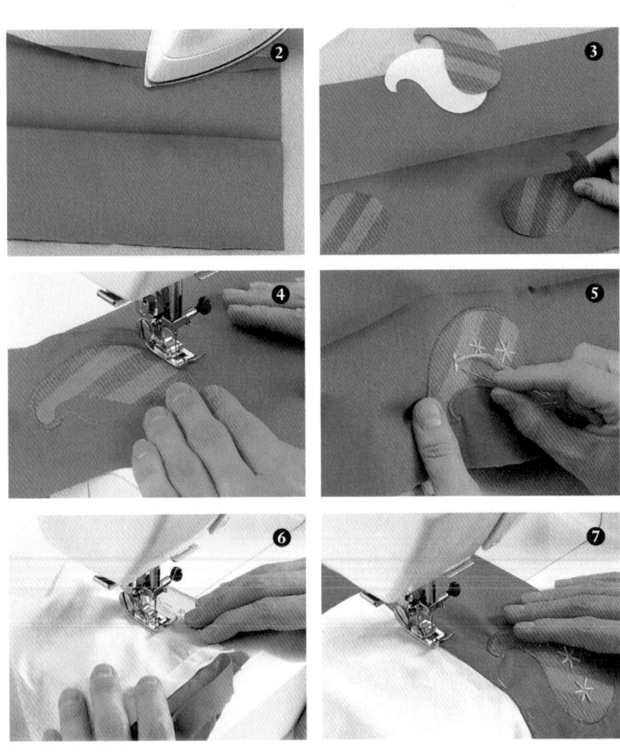

# comforter cover with ties

Make a feature of the fastening on a comforter cover with a row of pretty ties across the top of the cover. A generous flap is made from classic, checkered gingham with matching ties. Gingham is a cheap fabric to buy, and most of the comforter cover is made from inexpensive sheeting.

## Making a single comforter cover with ties

1 *Cut a front 76 x 56¼ in/1930 x 1425mm and a back 280 x 56¼ in/2035 x 1425mm from plain sheeting fabric. Press ¾ in/15mm under, then 2in/50mm on one short edge of the front. Stitch close to the inner pressed edge.*

2 *Cut ten 4⅜ in/110mm wide strips of gingham for the ties 10⅝ in/270mm long. Fold lengthwise in half with the right sides facing, and cut diagonally across one end. Stitch the outer edges, taking a ⅜ in/10mm seam allowance, leaving a 3in/75mm gap to turn through. Clip the corners, turn right side out, and press. Slipstitch the openings closed.*

3 *Cut a strip of gingham fabric 56¼ x 21¼ in/1425 x 540mm for the flap. Press the flap lengthwise in half with the wrong sides facing. Pin the raw edges together. Mark the center with a row of pins parallel with the short edges. Pin one tie to the center line, with the tie extending over the fold the the straight end 2in/50mm from the fold.*

4 *Baste the remaining ties to the flap 8¼ in/205mm apart. Stitch in place close to the edges and across the tie at the straight end, forming a 1½ in/38mm square. Stitch a cross formation within the square.*

5 *With the wrong sides facing, pin the front to the back, matching the short lower and long side raw edges. Pin the flap on top. The seams are stitched with a French seam. Stitch the outer edges, taking a ¼ in/6mm seam allowance. Clip the corners. Turn wrong side out and stitch again, taking a ⅜ in/10mm seam allowance. Turn right side out. Pin the remaining ties to the front 4¾ in/120mm from the lower edge of the flap.*

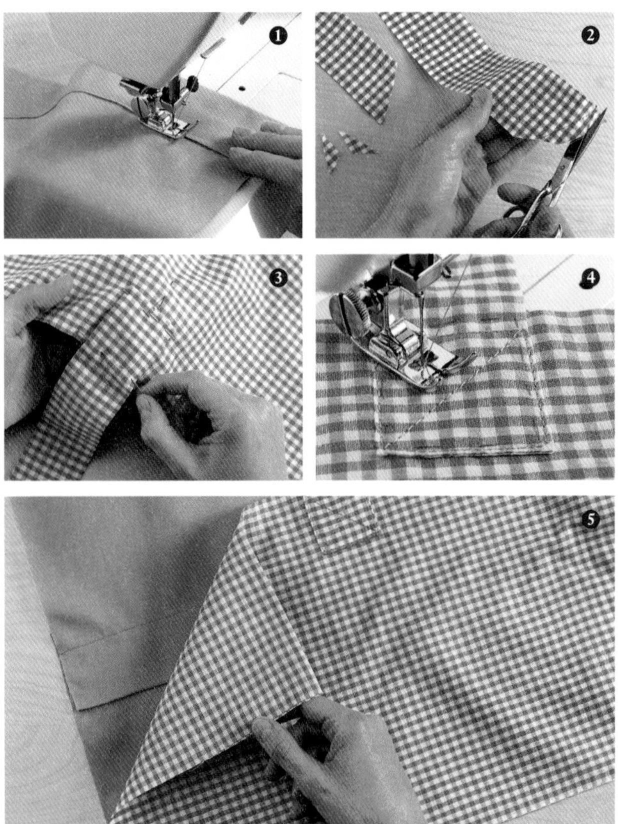

## Making a double comforter cover with ties

Cut a front 76 x 80in/1930 x 2035mm and a back 80 x 56¼ in/2035 x 1425mm. Cut a strip of fabric 80 x 21¼ in/2035 x 540mm for the flap and cut fourteen ties. Make a double comforter cover in the same way as a single one.

# pillowcases

Pillowcases lend themselves to many decorative features, and you can really go to town if you are handy with your needle. Decorate the edges of pillowcases with ribbons or lace, or work a design in fine embroidery silk. You can also experiment with fabric paints and pens, which can be used over the whole of the pillow.

A housewife pillowcase has a flap to hold the pillow in place, and supports the head whilst sleeping. A pillow sham is a pillow cover for a decorative pillow, or for back support. Pillow shams that are to be propped upright often have decorative borders, scalloped or flat, or frills extending beyond three edges. The fourth, lower edge conceals the fastening. Pillow shams are made in the same way as cushions, but do not have zipper fastenings.

The size of a pillowcase provides an ideal opportunity for decoration. Apply the decoration to the front before it is made up. Position any motifs about 2in/50mm in from the flap and up from the lower edge so they do not get lost over the curve of the pillow. Avoid placing any decoration other than fabric painting on the center of the pillowcase, because it could irritate the sleeper. A little lavender oil sprinkled on the pillow will aid peaceful sleep.

***There are many ways of decorating pillowcases and pillow shams, including embroidery.***

## Making a housewife pillowcase

*1 To make a standard-size housewife pillowcase, cut a front 38 x 20¼in/965 x 516mm and a back 31⅜ x 20¼in/795 x 516mm. Press ⅜in/10mm under, then 1⅝in/40mm on one short edge of the front and back. Stitch close to the inner pressed edges.*

*2 With right sides facing, pin the front and back together along the remaining short edges. Fold the other end of the front over to form a flap, then pin the layers together.*

*3 Stitch the raw edges together, taking a ⅝in/15mm seam allowance. Clip the corners. Neaten the seam with a zigzag stitch or pinking shears. Turn right side out, turning the flap inside.*

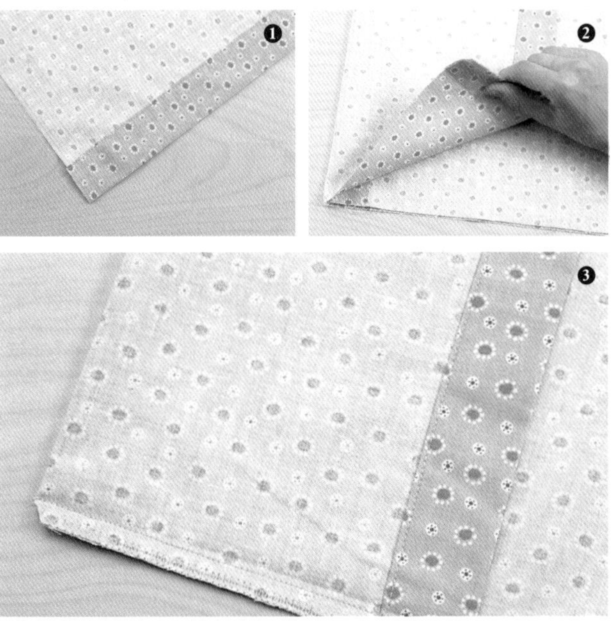

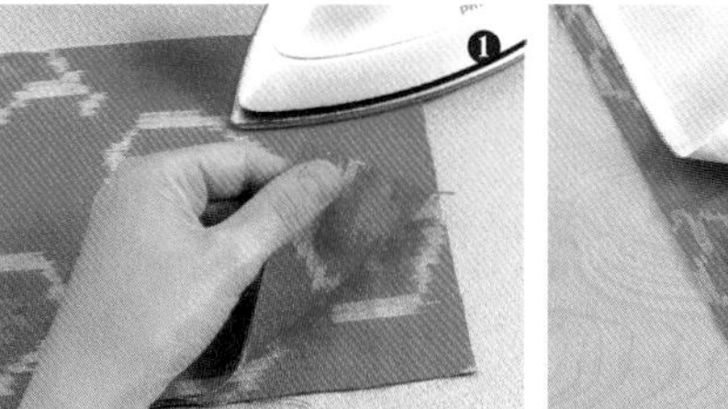

## Making a decorative flap housewife pillowcase

This version of a housewife pillowcase has a flap that closes over the front of the pillowcase; this can be of a contrasting color or fabric to the pillowcase, or decorated with all sorts of techniques, or fastened with buttons and buttonholes. The buttonholes are worked on the flap.

*1 Cut a front and back 36¼ x 20¼in/790 x 516mm. Cut a flap 9 x 20¼in/225 x 516mm. Press ⅜in/10mm under, then ⅝in/15mm on one short edge of the front, and stitch close to the inner pressed edges. Press the flap in half with right sides facing, parallel with the long edges. If you wish to decorate the flap, open it out flat and apply the decoration to one half only.*

*2 With right sides facing, baste the raw edges of the flap to one end of the back.*

*3 With right sides facing, pin the front on top, with the hemmed edge over the flap. Stitch the outer edges, taking a ⅝in/15mm seam allowance. Clip the corners. Neaten with a zigzag stitch or pinking shears. Turn right side out, turning the flap over the front.*

# bedspreads

Because a bedspread covers such a large expanse, it will be a major focal point of the bedroom. Bedspreads are a great way of either creating a dramatic effect with a bright splash of color in an otherwise subtle room, or of calming down a color scheme by making the bedspread in gentle, soothing tones.

From a practical point of view, a bedspread will add warmth and hide dreary blankets. It will also hide the bed base and anything stored under it, making a bed valance unnecessary.

A throw-over bedspread is very simple to make because it is just a rectangle of fabric that is large enough to reach the floor at the sides and foot of the bed. It can be a single layer of fabric, or it can be lined. A contrasting colored lining makes the bedspread reversible, which is very versatile. On a single layer bedspread, add a 1in/25mm hem to all edges or, alternatively, bind the edges, in which case no allowances are needed. Lined bedspreads can also have bound edges, or add a 5/8in/15mm seam allowance to all edges if you prefer to bag it out. Most fabrics are suitable, but avoid any that are stiff, because the bedspread will not drape nicely over the bed. If lining the bedspread, make sure the fabrics have compatible care instructions.

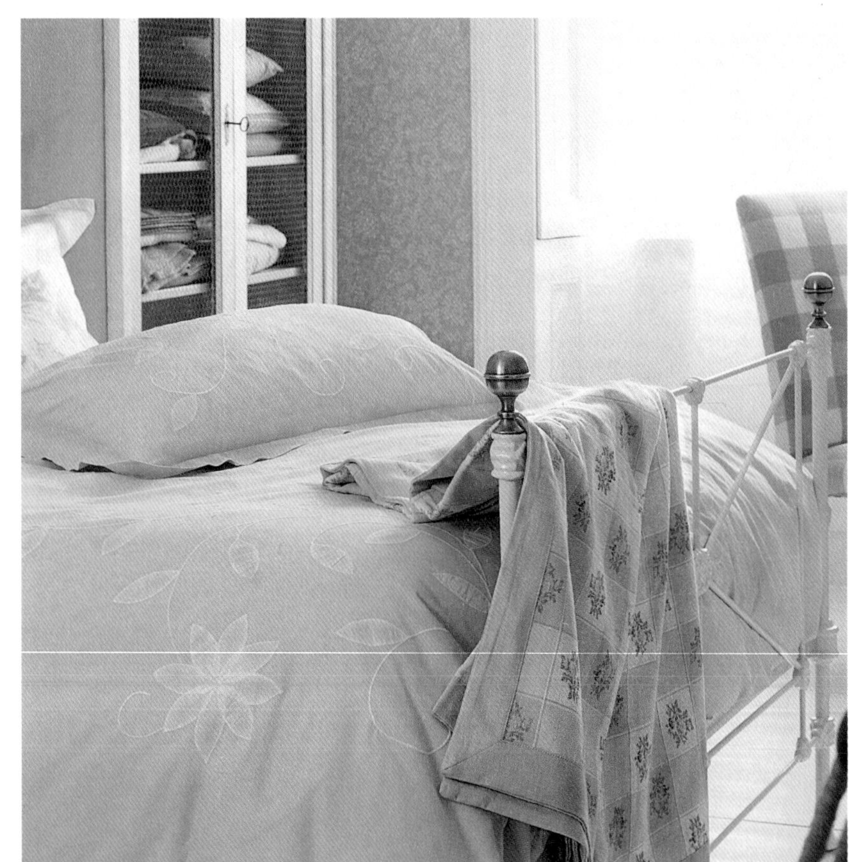

### *Joining widths*

The large size of a bedspread means that fabric will probably need to be joined to achieve the required width. As on curtains and tablecloths, a central join will look ugly, so try to have a full width of fabric along the center of the length of the bed and an equal amount of fabric at each side. Making the central panel from a contrasting fabric to those at each side can be very effective. Add 5/8in/15mm seam allowances for joining the widths. Use flat felled seams on single layer bedspreads, and flat seams on lined bedspreads. The corners at the foot end will need to be rounded off on a floor-length bedspread, otherwise they will bunch up on the floor and could be tripped over.

***A bedspread needs to be made from a fabric that hangs well when draped over a bed. The color can create either a dramatic or a soothing effect.***

## Making a throw-over bedspread with bound edges

To measure for a throw-over bedspread, make up the bed in your usual way, complete with pillows and comforter or blankets. With a tape measure, measure the width from the floor at one side of the bed, up over the bed, and to the floor at the other side. Measure the length from the floor at the foot of the bed, up and along the length of the bed, over the pillows to the headboard. If you require a tuck-in under the pillows, add 16in/405mm to the length. Add a 1in/25mm hem to the head end.

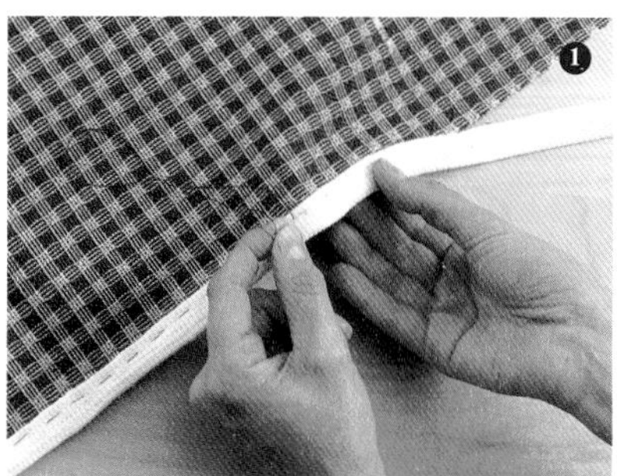

*1 Cut out the bedspread. Join the widths, matching patterns if necessary. Press under 3/8in/10mm then 5/8in/15mm on the head end. Stitch close to the inner pressed edge. Fold the bedspread lengthwise in half with the right sides facing. Measure the height of the made-up bed. On paper, use a pair of tool compasses to describe a quarter circle with a radius that is the bed height measurement. Cut out the quarter circle pattern, and pin it to the foot end corners. Cut around the curves.*

*2 Remove the pattern and open the bedspread out flat. Open out a length of fold-over braid and turn under one end. Starting at the hemmed edge, slot the raw edge of the bedspread into the braid. Baste in place, through all the layers, enclosing the raw edges. Turn under the extending end to finish. Stitch close to the inner edges of the braid through all the layers, then carefully remove all the basting.*

# pillow shams and cushions

Pillow shams are used to lean on when you sit up in bed—cushions are generally more decorative, but can also be used for the same purpose. Don't be mean with cushions, pile them up generously, and let them spill over the bed to create an inviting atmosphere. Use luxurious fabrics for that feel-good factor.

A pile of squashy pillows and cushions on a bed looks very cosy and welcoming. Pillows and cushions are easy to make and offer lots of opportunities for trying out different needlecraft techniques. If you wish to add trimmings, such as fringing or beading, to the outer edges, apply these to three sides only—pillow shams are traditionally meant to sit upright to support the back, so any trimming on the lower edge would be squashed and hidden from view.

The traditional craft of patchwork has long been associated with making beautiful heirloom quilts for the bedroom. They are time-consuming and labor-intensive to create, but a work of art when completed. Making a patchwork pillow sham is a much simpler process, as well as being a great introduction to the technique. Patchwork is a super way to use up small pieces of fabric and those that have sentimental value. Choose fabrics of similar weight: lightweight interfacing can be applied to the back of very fine or unstable fabrics to give them more body. Baste lightweight sew-in interfacing to the back of a piece of lace, a worn fabric from a favorite dress you want to incorporate for sentimental reasons, or a delicate piece of an antique textile.

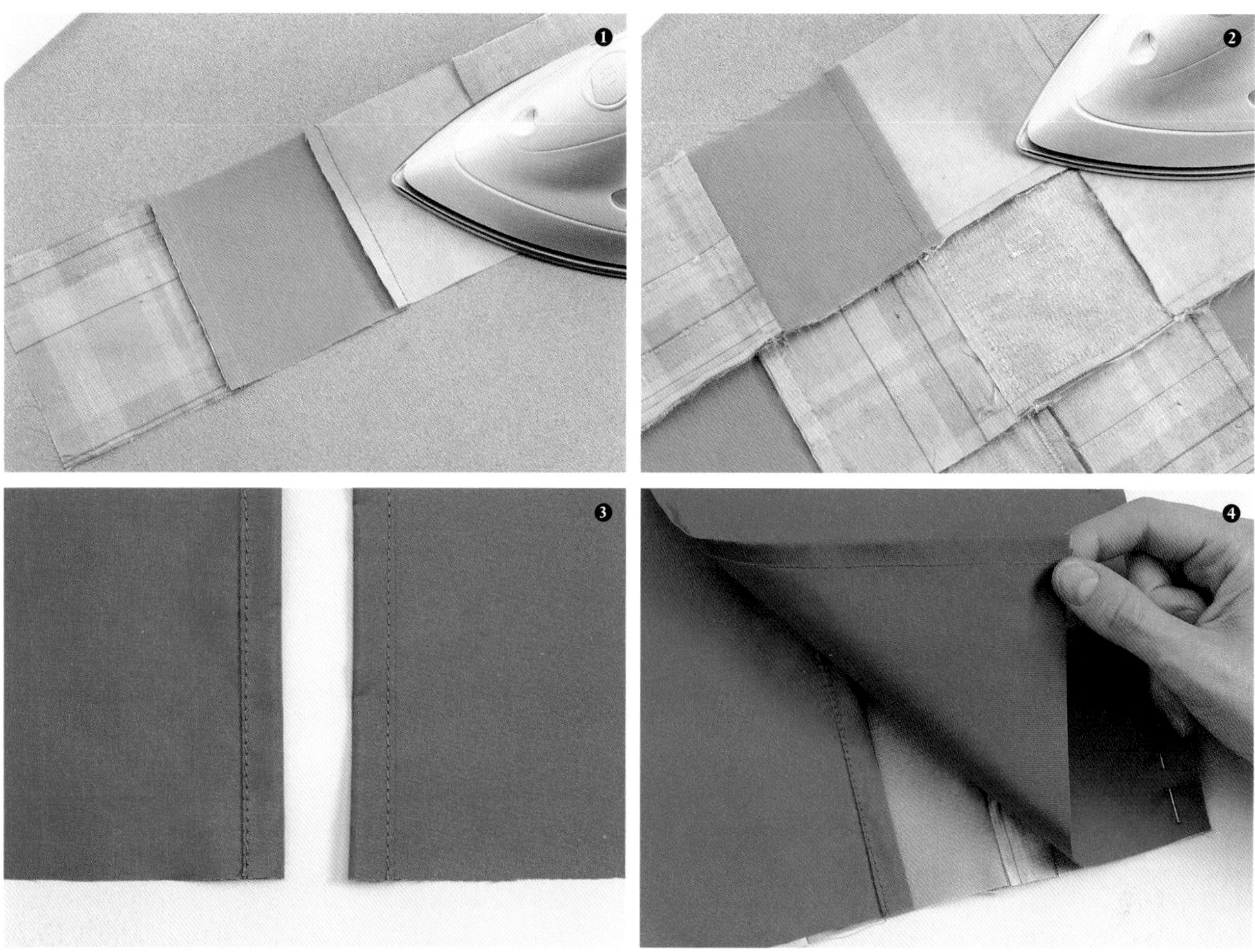

## Making a patchwork pillow sham

The finished size of the pillow sham is 12in/305mm square. Take ⅜in/10mm seam allowances throughout. The patchwork is machine stitched using silk fabrics in co-ordinating colors. The seams are outlined with rows of shiny sequins.

1 *Cut sixteen 3¾in/95mm squares from four co-ordinating fabrics. Arrange the squares in different sequences of four rows of four squares to see what looks best. With the right sides facing, stitch the four squares together in four rows. Press the seams of the first row in the same direction, the seams of the next row in the opposite direction, and so on.*

2 *With the right sides facing, stitch the first two rows together, matching the seams. Join the remaining rows to form a square for the front of the sham. Press the seams downwards.*

3 *Cut two rectangles of fabric for the back 8½ x 12¾in/215 x 325mm. Press a ⅜in/10mm deep double hem under on one long edge of each piece, and stitch in place.*

4 *With the right sides facing, pin the backs to the front, matching the raw edges and overlapping the hems at the center. Stitch the outer edges. Clip the corners and turn right side out. Handsew a string of iridescent sequins along each seam, then slip a 12in/305mm cushion pad inside.*

# corona

Coronas make an attractive addition to any bedroom, and they will create a cosy atmosphere around your bed. They can be simple to put up, though—to quickly create a gauzy corona, fix a mosquito net above the bed. Use fabric glue to stick silk flower heads or silk leaves at random to the fabric.

Bed curtains were traditionally used for functional purposes only—to maintain privacy, and to keep out draughts. In the nineteenth century, heavily curtained four-poster beds were thought to be unhealthy, and the half-tester became the popular alternative. The half-tester is a rectangular canopy at the head end of the bed only, and will keep out draughts while adding a traditional and aristocratic feel to a bedroom. A corona has a curved board with curtains attached that are draped to either side of the bed; it has a softer look than a half-tester, and lends itself to both traditional and contemporary styles.

The corona curtains are attached with hooks to screw eyes fixed to the underside of a corona board. The board can have a pelmet attached and curtains with a standard heading underneath, or no pelmet and curtains with a pencil pleat heading. The curtains can continue behind the head end of the bed, in which case it would be best to line them, maybe in a co-ordinating, plain fabric.

***There are several variations that can be made on this style of corona, including hanging curtains behind the head of the bed, which should be lined with a co-ordinating plain fabric.***

## Making a corona

This corona has a matching pelmet with unlined curtains edged in braid.

1 *Cut a 24in/610mm diameter semicircle of ⅝in/15mm thick plywood for the corona board. Cut a 28in/710mm diameter semicircle of fabric. Place the corona centrally on the wrong side of the fabric. Working outward from the center, lift the edges of the fabric over the corona board and staple in place with a staple gun, folding under the fulness at the corners.*

2 *Staple a length of touch-and-close tape to the curved edge with a staple gun. Screw an L-shape bracket to the top of the corona board on the straight edge, 4in/10mm in from the ends.*

3 *On the underside of the corona board, make an even number of holes with a bradawl ⅜in/10mm in from each corner, then approximately 1½in/40mm apart, ⅜in/10mm within the curved edge. Fix a screw eye into each hole, with the eyes parallel to the curved edge. Attach the corona board centrally above the bed. If the windows in the bedroom have a pelmet, match the height of the corona board with that of the pelmet shelf if possible.*

4 *Measure the length of the curve of the semicircle. Cut a 4in/100mm wide strip of self-adhesive pelmet interfacing the length of the curve. Cut two strips of fabric for the pelmet, adding a ⅝in/15mm allowance on each edge. Peel the paper backing off one side, and stick it centrally to one strip of fabric.*

5 *Cut diagonally across the fabric ¼in/6mm from the corners of the pelmet. Peel away the pelmet backing paper from the edges, and press the corners, then the straight edges of the fabric to the back of the pelmet.*

6 *For the lining, pin the corresponding half of the touch-and-close tape 1in/25mm below the upper long edge of the remaining strip of fabric, ⅝in/15mm in from the short edges. Stitch in place close to the edges of the tape. Press under ⅝in/15mm on the edges of the fabric.*

7 *Peel off the backing paper completely. Press the lining smoothly on top. Slipstitch together along the outer edges. Handsew or glue a decorative trim along the lower edge of the pelmet. Press the pelmet to the corona, matching the touch-and-close tapes.*

8 *Use a tape measure to measure the intended drop of the curtains from the underside of the corona to the floor. Refer to the unlined curtain instructions on pages 34–35 to make a pair of curtains, each the length of the pelmet in width. Stitch a decorative trim along the inner edges if you wish. Use standard curtain tape for the curtain heading.*

9 *Slip curtain hooks through the tape, and slot the hooks through the eyelets on the underside of the corona. Fix a curtain boss or holdback either side of the bed to keep the curtains in place.*

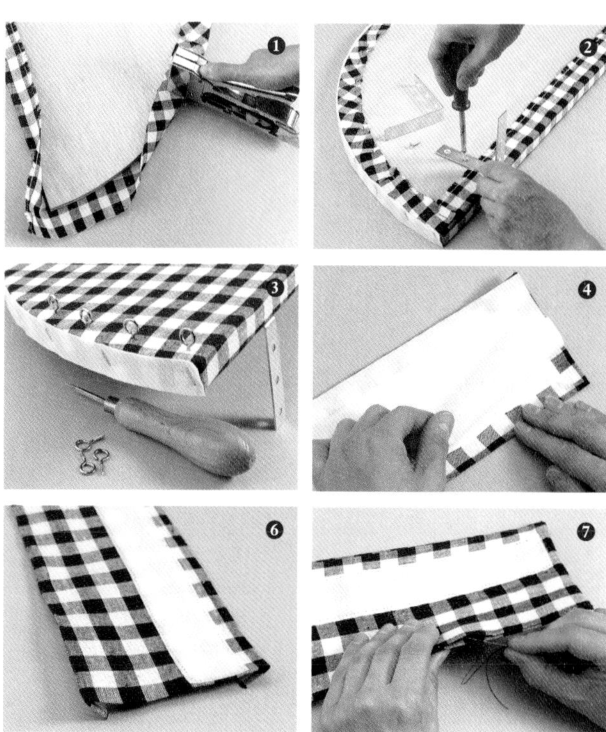

# index